MARIA WATKINS

HOPE *yet* AGAIN

HOPE ISN'T LOST - IT'S JUST WAITING FOR YOU TO BELIEVE AGAIN

1st edition 2024

Paperback ISBN: 979-8-9921279-3-5
E-Book ISBN: 979-8-9921279-2-8

Book Launch Publishing
booklaunchpub.com

Dedication

I am pleased to dedicate this to my precious sons, Bentley and Carson—this book is for you. You are the treasures of my heart, and I see God's hand in your lives every single day. You are my daily reminder of God's faithfulness, and my constant inspiration to keep my eyes fixed on Jesus. Watching you grow into the incredible young men God is shaping you to be fills me with hope and gratitude beyond words. As you grow wiser, you are navigating through a world that can feel uncertain and overwhelming at times. However, my prayer is that you always know how deeply you are loved and how you are uniquely designed for a purpose far greater than you can begin to imagine.

Hope Yet Again, is my legacy to you, born out of love, faith, and the desire to see you live boldly in God's promises. May it remind you to anchor your hope in Him, to trust His plans even when the way seems unclear, and to walk confidently into the future He has prepared for you. You are my greatest joy, my endless pride, and the reason I rise each day with faith in my heart. Thank you for praying for me; God has heard your prayers. I love you more.

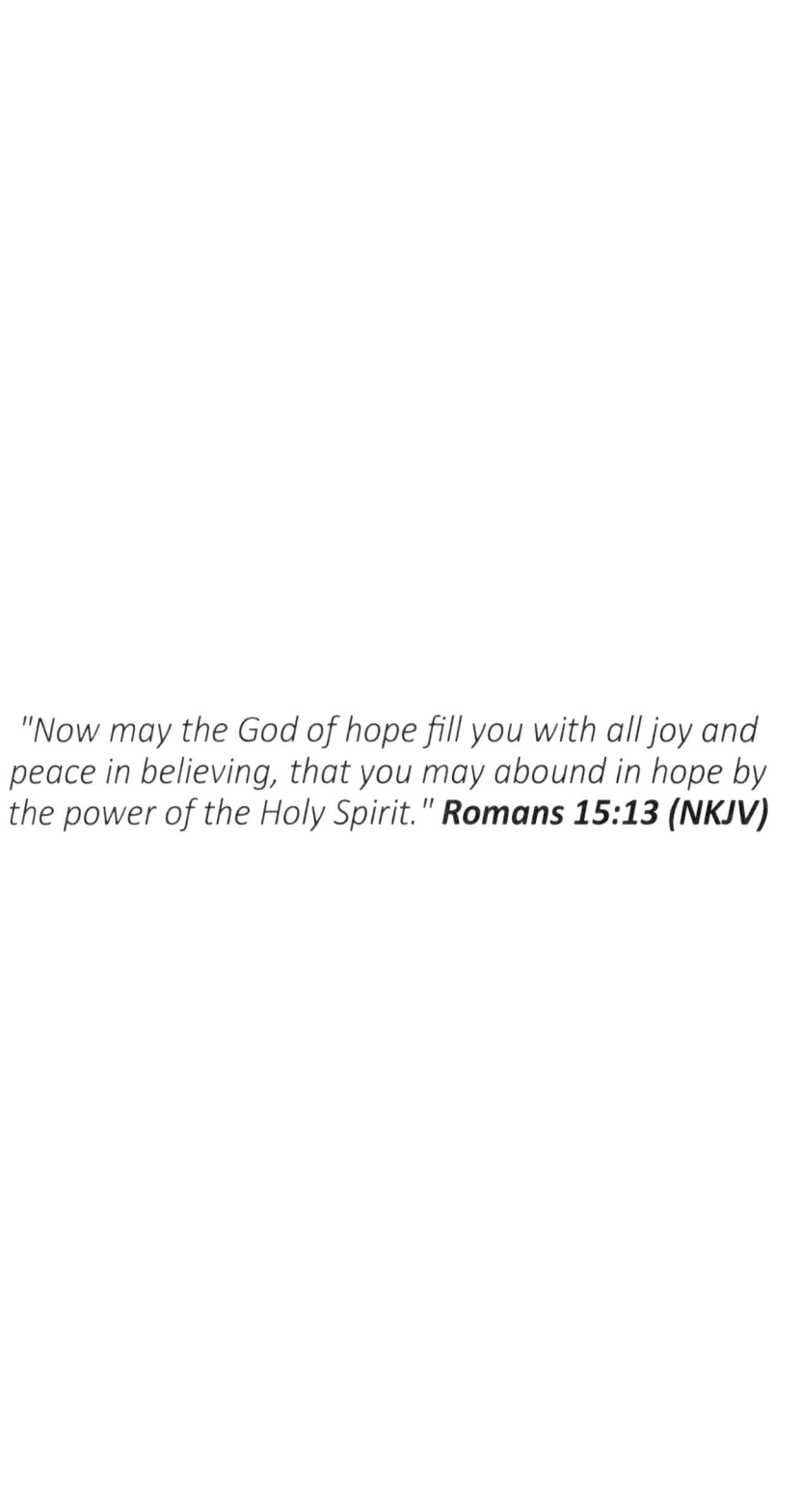

"Now may the God of hope fill you with all joy and peace in believing, that you may abound in hope by the power of the Holy Spirit." **Romans 15:13 (NKJV)**

Contents

Introduction

Have you ever felt like you're holding on to hope with nothing but a frayed thread, just wondering how long you can keep it together? Maybe you've been praying and believing, even begging for a breakthrough, but all you're met with is silence. If that's you, let me start by saying: I see you! You are not alone, and this book was written with you in mind.

Life has a way of throwing curveballs that make us question everything—our purpose, our strength, and sometimes even God's promises. Deferred hope can feel like a weight you weren't built to carry, but I want you to know something powerful: this season of waiting is not the end of your story. The fact that you're here, holding this book, tells me that deep down, you still believe in something greater. Let me tell you—you're right.

This book isn't just a collection of stories and principles; it's a journey for rediscovering the hope you thought was gone. It's about finding light in the darkness, clarity in the confusion, and strength in the struggle. It's a reminder that God's timing is never off, even when life feels like it's running way behind schedule.

Let's be real for a second—waiting can feel like standing in the world's longest line with no guarantee of what's at the front. But what if the waiting isn't punishment? What if it's preparation? What if God is using this very moment to shape you for something you can't even begin to imagine yet?

Throughout these pages, I'll share stories of heartache and triumph, moments of doubt and faith, and everything in between.

We'll walk through biblical truths that will challenge your perspective and ignite your faith. I'll even share some of my own messy, raw, and very real journey. I've been through seasons where hope felt like a cruel joke, where the weight of waiting seemed unbearable. But God... Oh, how He showed up in ways I couldn't have planned if I had tried.

Here's the thing—this book isn't just about me. It's about you. It's for the man or woman who's been battling silently, holding on when everything in you wants to let go. It's for the person who feels unseen, forgotten, or just plain exhausted. It's for anyone who needs to know that God still sees, still hears, and still cares deeply about every part of your life.

So, what's in this book? Stories of hope restored, decisions made in faith, promises fulfilled, and victories won. It's a roadmap to rediscovering God's purpose for your life and embracing the abundant hope He alone always offers. I won't just tell you what God has done— I'll invite you to see what He's ready to do in your own life.

I won't pretend this book will solve all your problems. However, I will promise this: if you lean into the pages, you'll find encouragement, guidance, and maybe even a laugh or two along the way. More importantly, you'll find a God who is faithful to finish what He starts.

You don't have to live in defeat. You don't have to carry the weight alone. And you don't have to stay stuck. Your story isn't over— this is just the beginning. So, take a deep breath, turn the page, and let's rediscover hope together because with God, the best is yet to come. Always.

Chapter One

HOPE RESTORED – REDISCOVERING THE LIGHT

How many times have you felt like the light has gone out within your life? Maybe you're trying to stand in the middle of a season where every morning seems the same. The weight of hopelessness lingers, and each step forward feels like you are wading through thick mud. Here's the hard truth—sometimes, even those of us with strong faith feel like we're holding on only by a thread. Yet, here's the most beautiful truth of all: **hope in Christ isn't just a feeling. It's an unshakeable reality!**

In moments when life's circumstances cast long shadows over our hearts, it's easy to think that hope has completely vanished. We tend to look at our past failures, our present struggles, or an uncertain future, and the burden can actually feel crushing. I want to remind you that even in the darkest moments, there's a light that never fades. Christ Himself promises us that He is our light, even when we feel totally surrounded by darkness.

The Biblical Example of Job

No one knew darkness like Job. He lost everything—his wealth, his family, and even his health. His life went from abundance to ashes in what must have felt like an instant. Job could have stayed in despair, consumed by the unfairness of it all. What makes his story so remarkable though is that he didn't let the darkness define him.

In **Job 19:25 (NIV)**, despite his pain, Job declared: *"I know that my redeemer lives, and that in the end he will stand on the earth."* Job chose to cling to hope, even when his circumstances screamed otherwise. Job's perseverance eventually paid off. God not only restored what was lost but also blessed Job with even more than he had before. Job's story teaches us that even when we feel like we're at the end, God is only just beginning.

My Journey to Rediscover the Light

Let me take you to a season in my life that felt uncertain, overwhelming, and downright terrifying. After my divorce, I found myself in a position I never expected—needing a job after being out of the workforce for over eight years. For nearly a decade, my entire world had revolved around my family. However, now I faced the daunting task of providing for my boys while still being the present, deeply involved mother they deserved. The weight of responsibility was heavy, and the path ahead felt anything but clear.

The job I needed wasn't just about making ends meet. It had to be flexible enough to allow me to drop off and pick up my boys from school, attend their events, and still provide financially for our needs. To make things even more complicated, I didn't have a single clue as to where I should start. How do you step into the unknown when the path ahead seems invisible?

Through it all, my hope was in the Lord. Every day, I prayed to Him, bringing Him all my uncertainty, my fears, and my overwhelming need for direction. I didn't know what His plan looked like, but I chose to believe He had one. I leaned on **Proverbs 3:5-6**, trusting in His understanding and not my own. It wasn't easy to see what He was doing, but I held on to the truth that all I had to do was believe—and let Him take care of the rest.

> *I didn't know what His plan looked like, but I chose to believe He had one.*

One day, while hosting a Bible study at my house, one of my friends walked in and without hesitation asked: "Do you need a job?"

I was stunned. I just stared at her for a moment before blurting out, "Yes! How did you know?" She smiled knowingly and replied, "Just send me your resume, and I'll make sure it gets into the right hands."

The problem? I didn't have a resume. I did not even have a rough draft. But that same afternoon, I sat down and pieced something together, and sent it off to her. To my amazement, things started falling into place almost immediately. I landed a job that fit perfectly with my schedule, allowing me to be there for my boys and provide for them at the same time. If that wasn't enough, the job also gave me the ability to buy a vehicle—another answered prayer I hadn't seen coming.

God came through in ways I couldn't have orchestrated even if I tried. He made a way where there seemed to be no way. Looking back, I see His hand in every detail: the timing, the opportunity, the provision—it was all Him. What felt impossible became possible because I chose to trust Him, even when I couldn't see how it would all work out.

This experience taught me that hope isn't just a feeling; it's a choice. It's deciding to believe in God's faithfulness, even when circumstances look unfavorable. It's leaning on His understanding and trusting that His plan is far better than anything we could imagine. Through every prayer and every step of faith, despite moments of uncertainty, I discovered that God's light shines brightest in the darkness. All we have to do is believe.

Biblical Principles for Rediscovering the Light

1. **Seek God in Every Season:** Like Job, we need to keep our eyes on God, even when life feels unbearable. **Psalm 34:17 (NIV)** reminds us, *"The righteous cry out, and the LORD hears them; he delivers them from all their troubles."* God is always near, ready to guide us towards hope.

2. **Be Willing to Step Forward in Faith:** Sometimes, the hardest part is taking the first step. Whether it's dusting off an old resume or stepping into an unfamiliar situation, faith requires action. **James 2:26 (NKJV)** says, *"faith without works is dead."* God moves when we do.

3. **Trust That God's Plans Are Perfect:** You may not see how everything will come together, but God does. **Proverbs 3:5-6 (NIV)** teaches us to; *"Trust in the LORD with all your heart and lean not on your own understanding."* His way is always better.

4. **Cling to the Light of His Word:** When life feels dark, God's Word becomes our flashlight. **Psalm 119:105 (NKJV)** reminds us, *"Your word is a lamp to my feet, and a light to my path."* Immerse yourself in His promises—they'll guide you to the next step.

Laughter and Light

Life has a funny way of throwing curveballs that can either knock you down or leave you laughing at the absurdity of it all. Sometimes, the best remedy for a heavy heart is a little humor. Like the time I tried to piece together a resume after eight years out of the workforce while simultaneously stopping my kids from "redecorating" the living room with playdoh. It wasn't pretty, but it was real—and looking back, it's hilarious.

Here's the truth: God's not sitting up in heaven, shaking His head at your struggles. He's with you, smiling as you fumble your way through, cheering you on with every little victory. **Proverbs 17:22 (NIV)** reminds us, *"A cheerful heart is good medicine,"* and it's true. Laughter doesn't fix everything, but it has a way of lightening the load just enough for us to take the next step.

So, go ahead—find the humor in the journey. Let yourself laugh at the absurdity of it all, because sometimes laughter is the light we need to rediscover hope. After all, God didn't bring you this far to leave you without joy along the way. In fact, the joy of the Lord is your strength according to **Nehemiah 8:10**.

If Job's story—and mine—teach us anything, it's this: God is faithful. He is the light that leads us through every valley, the provider who meets every need, and the restorer of all that feels lost. No matter where you are today, remember this: the light is never gone—it's just waiting for you to look up and rediscover it.

Take that step of faith. Trust that God is working behind the scenes. If all else fails, remember: if He can create the universe in six days, He can handle whatever you're facing today. The light is coming—it's time for you to walk towards it.

A Prayer for Rediscovering the Light

Lord, thank You for being our light in the darkness, our hope in despair, and our guide when life feels uncertain. Help us to trust You, even when the path ahead seems unclear. Teach us to take steps of faith, knowing that You are always working for our good. Thank You for Your promises and for the joy that comes when we lean into You. Amen.

Chapter Two

FROM HELPLESSNESS TO STRENGTH – EMBRACING GOD'S POWER

Have you ever felt trapped by your own circumstances, like everything around you was falling apart and there was nothing you could do? Perhaps you felt like the life you knew was slipping away, piece by piece, leaving you wondering where to go next. Helplessness can be one of the most painful feelings, pulling us into a place of loneliness, doubt, and fear. However, here's the truth: the very moments that strip us of our self-reliance are often the ones where God's strength becomes the most real.

The Bible is filled with reminders of God's strength when we feel weakest. Think of Paul's words in **2 Corinthians 12:9 (NIV)** where the Lord told him: *"My grace is sufficient for you, for my power is made perfect in weakness."* God's strength doesn't just compensate for our weakness; it shines best in our weakest moments, turning the places of brokenness into testimonies of His goodness. That very same power is available to you, right where you are.

Gideon's Journey from Helplessness to Strength

I am reminded of the story of Gideon, a man who also felt small and helpless. The Israelites were being oppressed by the Midianites, who destroyed their land and left them struggling to survive. Gideon, feeling weak and insignificant, was hiding in a winepress, threshing wheat while hidden from the enemy. In his heart, he probably felt that nothing he could do would make a difference. Yet, it was in that hidden, fearful place that God found him.

When the angel of the Lord appeared to Gideon, he greeted him with these words: *"The LORD is with you, mighty warrior"* **Judges 6:12 (NIV)**. Can you imagine how Gideon must have felt hearing that? There he was, hiding out, feeling inadequate and fearful, and yet God saw something more—a mighty warrior. God looked beyond Gideon's fear and saw his potential, the strength that could emerge when empowered by the Almighty.

Gideon (like many of us) struggled to believe that he could overcome his circumstances. He questioned, he doubted, and he needed reassurance. God, with infinite patience and kindness, met him right in that place of doubt. Through a series of signs, God reminded Gideon that He was with him, that His strength would be sufficient for the impossible task ahead.

So, with only 300 men Gideon went on to lead Israel to a miraculous victory over the Midianites. God showed Gideon that His power is always greater than the odds stacked against us. It wasn't Gideon's strength that won the battle; it was God's strength working through him.

My Journey from Helplessness to Strength

I remember a season in my life when helplessness felt like a constant shadow over me. I was going through a painful divorce, something I had never imagined for myself. Each day felt like an uphill battle—not only was I navigating the emotional pain of separation, but I was also facing financial struggles, wondering how I'd ever make ends meet for myself and my children. The weight of hopelessness was real, and it threatened to swallow me whole. I felt trapped, as if my circumstances were walls closing in on me, blocking every path forward.

One night, I found myself pouring my heart out to God, letting out all the fears and tears I'd previously kept inside. In that moment, a simple yet profound truth settled over me: I didn't have to be strong on my own. God was offering me His strength, His comfort, and His guidance in a way I had never experienced before. Slowly, day by day, I began to lean on Him, more and more, taking each small step with the assurance that I wasn't alone. As I let go of my need to control things and surrendered my fears to Him, I discovered a strength I didn't know I had—His strength flowing through me.

Through this experience, I realized that sometimes, God allows us to reach the end of our own strength so that we can fully experience His. He showed me that, even in the most difficult seasons, His grace is more than enough. If He could carry me through that valley, I knew He could carry me through anything.

> *God allows us to reach the end of our own strength so that we can fully experience His.*

My circumstances didn't change overnight, but I could feel God lifting the weight of them off of my heart, replacing my fear with faith, and my hopelessness with courage. This was a journey of surrender—learning that God's strength could carry me through valleys I could never cross alone. Like a flickering light, hope began to be rekindled within me, and I knew I wasn't walking this path alone.

Finding Strength in Our Weakness

Both my story and Gideon's journey illustrate this incredible truth: when we reach the end of our own strength, we find that God's strength is more than enough. We may feel like we have nothing to offer, that the battle is too big or the circumstances too overwhelming, but God sees what we cannot. He sees the potential within us, just waiting to be unleashed by His power.

So, when you feel helpless, remember this: you are not alone, and you don't have to be strong on your own. Like Gideon, you are a "mighty warrior," even if you don't feel like one. God's strength is made perfect in our weakness **2 Corinthians 12:9**, and He is more than able to carry us through any valley. Trust in His promises, lean into His power, and let Him transform your helplessness into unshakeable strength.

How to Overcome Helplessness Using Biblical Principles

1. **Recognize Your True Source of Strength:** In moments of helplessness, it's tempting to rely on our own limited strength. But remember **Philippians 4:13 (NKJV)**: *"I can do all things through Christ who strengthens me."* Let this be your reminder that God's strength, not yours, is the foundation of overcoming anything.

2. **Surrender Your Fears in Prayer:** One of the first steps to breaking free from helplessness is learning to surrender every fear, every doubt, and every burden to God. **1 Peter 5:7 (NIV)** says, *"Cast all your anxiety on Him because He cares for you."* Pour your heart out to Him in prayer, trusting that He cares deeply for you and every concern you carry.

3. **Anchor Yourself in God's Promises:** When you're feeling weak, dig deep into God's Word. Verses like **Isaiah 40:29-31 (NIV)** remind us that: *"He gives strength to the weary and increases the power of the weak."* Fill your heart with these promises, letting them remind you of God's power and faithfulness.

4. **Take Small, Faith-Filled Steps:** Sometimes, breaking out of helplessness starts with the smallest steps of faith. Ask God for guidance on where to focus and what steps to take next. Trust Him with each action, knowing that He will meet you with strength and courage.

5. **Seek Encouragement from a Supportive Community:** You don't have to face this journey alone. Surround yourself with people who will lift you up, pray for you, and remind you of God's strength in your life. As **Proverbs 27:17 (NIV)** says, *"As iron sharpens iron, so one person sharpens another."*

As you step forward on your own journey from here, know this: God's strength is available to you in every moment of weakness. When you feel helpless, remember that He is your stronghold, your shield, and your unfailing source of courage. In Him, you'll find strength not just to survive but to overcome, to rise, and to embrace the future with renewed hope.

A Prayer for God's Strength

Father, I come to You feeling weak and burdened by the struggles I'm facing. I don't know how to move forward on my own, but I know that I don't have to. You are my strength, my refuge, and my help. Remind me each day that Your power is greater than my circumstances. Help me to surrender my fears, to trust in Your promises, and to take each step with faith. Thank You for carrying me when I can't carry myself. In Jesus' name, Amen.

Chapter Three

MOTIVATION FOR EVERY DAY – LIVING WITH PURPOSE

When life feels heavy, when loneliness creeps in, and when our sense of worth feels diminished, it can be difficult to find the motivation to move forward. We wonder why we even try, why we put in the effort, and why we continue pressing on when the days feel so empty. Let me tell you this: the motivation to live each day with purpose and intention comes from a profound truth—God has a unique destiny for each of us, a calling that reaches beyond ourselves and touches the lives of many others.

Finding the motivation to go on is often rooted in discovering our identity in Christ. We aren't here by accident, our lives are woven into a much larger, divine tapestry. When we understand that our destiny impacts not just ourselves but also those we're called to touch, every action takes on new meaning. Every step

Finding the motivation to go on is often rooted in discovering our identity in Christ.

forward, no matter how small, is a step towards fulfilling a purpose that goes far beyond our own lives.

Understanding Purpose Through Our Tests: The Story of Moses

Moses' life is a profound example of how God uses our trials and tests to reveal our purpose. Born during a time of great oppression, Moses narrowly escaped death as an infant and instead was raised in Pharaoh's palace—an unlikely beginning for the man who would lead the Israelites to freedom. Yet Moses' journey wasn't without its challenges.

After killing an Egyptian in an attempt to defend a fellow Hebrew, Moses fled to the wilderness where he spent 40 years tending sheep. Can you imagine what that must have felt like? He had gone from royalty to obscurity, and was most likely wrestling with feelings of failure and confusion about his place in the world. However, God was at work, even in the wilderness. Those years of quiet preparation were actually shaping Moses into the leader he would need to become.

When God finally called Moses through the burning bush in **Exodus 3**, Moses did not feel ready. He questioned his ability, his qualifications, and even God's plan. However, God's response was clear: *"I will be with you"* **Exodus 3:12 (NIV)**. Moses' purpose wasn't about his strength or qualifications; it was about God's presence and power working through him.

Moses went on to lead the Israelites out of Egypt, to part the Red Sea, and to receive the Ten Commandments. However, none of that would have happened if he hadn't trusted God enough to step into his calling. Moses' story reminds us that our purpose often comes from the very trials that seem to disqualify us. The years Moses spent in the wilderness weren't wasted—they were the training ground for his destiny.

Just like Moses, your trials are part of God's preparation for you. The challenges you've faced, the struggles you've endured, and the lessons you've learned are shaping you for the purpose God has designed for your life. The key is trusting Him and taking the next step, even when you feel unqualified. As Moses' story shows, it's not about what you can do—it's about what God can do through you.

My Journey to Find Purpose in God

There was a season in my life when feelings of loneliness and worthlessness seemed to press in on every side. It felt like I was merely existing, moving through the motions of life without any sense of purpose or significance. In those moments of despair, I turned to the Word of God, desperate for answers and a renewed sense of direction. What I found there changed everything!

As I read, God began to speak to my heart through His Word, whispering truths that pierced through the lies I had believed. One day, I distinctly felt Him whisper: *"You are not alone—you just feel lonely."* That truth struck me deeply, and it reminded me of His promise in **Deuteronomy 31:8 (NIV)**, *"The LORD himself goes before you and will be with you; he will never leave you nor forsake you."* I began to see that my feelings of isolation didn't define my reality—rather, His presence did.

Through the pages of Scripture, God reminded me of who I truly am in Him. **Isaiah 43:6b-7 (NIV)** became a beacon of hope: *"Bring my sons from afar and my daughters from the ends of the earth—everyone who is called by my name, whom I created for my glory, whom I formed and made."* That verse spoke to the very depths of my soul, reminding me that I was created for a purpose—to glorify Him. My worth wasn't tied to my circumstances or my struggles, but to the unshakable truth that I was lovingly made for God's purposes.

As this truth took root in my heart, I began to realize that my life wasn't just about me. My destiny was tied to something far greater—every person God had called me to impact. There were hearts waiting to be encouraged, souls needing restoration, and lives that could be transformed through the hope I had found in Him. The trials I had faced weren't wasted; they were preparation for the calling God had placed upon my life.

This understanding brought a profound shift in my motivation. I began to see my goals not as tasks to accomplish but as opportunities to align with God's purpose. I realized that my willingness to step into my calling wasn't just about my own fulfillment—it was about fulfilling His plan within the lives of others. Knowing that God had a purpose for my life reignited a passion within me to pursue my calling with faith and determination.

If you find yourself feeling lonely or questioning your worth, let me encourage you: you are not alone. God is with you, and He has never left your side. You were created for His glory, with a purpose that only you can fulfill. The trials you face today may be preparing you for the lives you are destined to touch tomorrow. Trust in His promises, lean into His Word, and take the next step in faith. You were made for this, and He will equip you every step of the way.

Living Each Day with Intentionality

Both Moses' story and my own journey have taught me a profound truth: our lives are not just for ourselves. Moses was called to lead the Israelites out of slavery, but his calling wasn't about his own comfort or success—it was about setting an entire nation free. In the same way, there are people waiting for us to step into our God-given destinies, waiting for the encouragement, hope, and love that God desires to deliver to them through us.

When we align our actions with the goals God has set for our lives, we begin to live with a motivation that goes far beyond personal achievement. Just as Moses' obedience impacted generations, our purpose is also tied to the lives we are called to influence. Our motivation shifts—it's no longer just about reaching our own goals, but about the lives that will be touched, transformed, and restored through our faithfulness to God's plan.

How to Overcome a Lack of Motivation Using Biblical Principles

1. **Anchor Your Identity in Christ:** Understanding who you are in Christ is foundational. Meditate on verses like **1 Peter 2:9 (NIV)** – *"But you are a chosen people, a royal priesthood, a holy nation, God's special possession"*. Let this scripture remind you that you are called, loved, and purposed for something greater than yourself.

2. **Seek God's Purpose in Your Goals:** Reflect on your goals and ask if they align with God's vision for your life. Ask yourself if there are people God is calling you to reach through your actions. **Proverbs 19:21 (NIV)** reminds us, *"Many are the plans in a person's heart, but it is the LORD's purpose that prevails."*

3. **Make Your Actions Count for Eternity:** Each day is an opportunity to make an eternal impact. Keep in mind the souls, lives, and hearts that God wants to reach through you. This perspective brings new meaning to every task, no matter how small.

4. **Draw Inspiration from Biblical Stories:** When your motivation wanes, turn to the stories of those who lived purposefully for God's call, like Moses or Paul. Their lives remind us that God empowers us to make a difference beyond ourselves.

5. **Surround Yourself with God-Centered Support:** Seek community that encourages you to pursue God's calling. As

Hebrews 10:24 (NIV) says, *"Let us consider how we may spur one another on toward love and good deeds"*

Living with purpose means moving beyond temporary motivations and stepping into a mission that touches eternity. Like Moses, we are called to rise up in the moments God has appointed, even when we feel unqualified or uncertain. Just as Moses was called to lead the Israelites to freedom, we are called to walk in obedience, trusting that God will use our lives to bless, uplift, and transform those around us. Let this be the heartbeat of your journey, propelling you forward each day with the assurance that your life holds divine significance and that every step of faith you take is never in vain.

A Prayer for Purpose and Motivation

Lord, I come to You seeking renewed motivation and purpose. I confess that sometimes I struggle to find meaning in my day-to-day actions. Remind me, Father, of who I am in You and of the calling You have placed on my life. Help me to align my goals with Your purposes, to live each day with intentionality, and to remember that my life is meant to touch the lives of others. Give me strength, courage, and passion to live fully for Your glory. In Jesus' name, Amen.

Chapter Four

HOPE DEFERRED BUT NOT DENIED – OVERCOMING DESPAIR

We've all felt the ache of waiting, that painful gap between a promise and its fulfillment. When hope is deferred, it's easy to feel as though the light at the end of the tunnel is too far away to reach. Yet, even in these seasons of waiting, God is working, shaping us, preparing us and equipping us for something far greater than we can even imagine. **Proverbs 13:12 (NIV)** tells us, *"Hope deferred makes the heart sick, but a longing fulfilled is a tree of life."* In these times of waiting, God's faithfulness is our anchor, holding us steady as we trust in His timing.

A Story of Hope Deferred: Abraham and Sarah

Abraham and Sarah know this journey of hope deferred well. God promised Abraham that he would become the father of many nations, yet years and years passed without a single child. Sarah felt the sting of disappointment as she waited for the promise to come to life. Days turned into years, and she began to doubt that God would fulfill His word. But God's timing was perfect. In their old age, against all odds, Sarah finally gave birth to Isaac, the child of God's promise. **Genesis 21:1-2 (NLT)** says, *"The LORD kept His word and did for Sarah exactly what He had promised."*

Abraham and Sarah's story is a reminder that God's promises are not constrained by time or circumstance. Even when hope feels distant, God's faithfulness remains. He is always at work, and His promises, though delayed, are never denied.

My Journey of Hope Deferred

In my own life, I have experienced the pain of hope deferred, particularly when it came to the promise of restoration for my family. God had given me a vision of healing and restoration for me and my boys, Bentley and Carson. We held onto that promise tightly, trusting that God would rebuild what was broken. But as the days turned into months, and months to years, the journey became one of trusting in His promises rather than focusing upon our current circumstances.

One of the most challenging aspects of this particular journey was transforming my mind to focus on God's truth rather than on what I could see or feel in the natural. It was a process of daily surrender, of choosing to believe in His faithfulness even when everything around me seemed uncertain. I had to anchor myself in His Word, reminding myself that His promises were unchanging, even when my circumstances were difficult.

Through this time of extreme testing, God began a deep healing process within my heart—and not just within mine but also within Bentley's and Carson's hearts as well. Every day, we faced the ache of unfulfilled promises, yet every day, Jesus met us there, guiding us into deeper intimacy with Him. This healing journey has been hard. It has meant allowing Jesus to strip away layers of pain, trauma, hurt, and hopelessness, peeling back everything that hindered us from receiving His love fully.

As Jesus worked in us, we experienced Him bringing purity and wholeness into places that had once been broken. Each tear, each prayer, and each moment of surrender brought us closer to Him. This has been one of the most intimate seasons of our lives, where we felt Jesus healing us not only as individuals, but as a family, drawing us into a unity that reflects His love. As He stripped away the brokenness, He replaced it with strength, with faith, and with a hope that has grown stronger with each passing day.

Though we haven't yet seen the complete restoration of our family, we know that God is faithful. This journey of waiting has become a journey of refining, where our intimacy with Jesus grows deeper and deeper each day. We are becoming the family He created us to be—filled with His love, standing on His promises, and walking in His purpose.

This journey of waiting has become a journey of refining, where our intimacy with Jesus grows deeper and deeper each day.

Biblical Principles to Overcome Despair in Seasons of Waiting

1. **Transform Your Mind by Trusting in God's Promises:** It's easy to be swayed by our circumstances, but God calls us to renew our minds daily through His Word. **Romans 12:2 (NIV)** urges, *"Do not conform to the pattern of this world, but be transformed by the renewing of your mind."* Focus on God's promises, and let them become the anchor for your thoughts.

2. **Allow God to Heal Your Heart and Release Past Hurts:** Waiting can bring unresolved pain to the surface. Allow God to heal those hidden wounds, bringing you to a place of peace. **Psalm 147:3 (NIV)** says, *"He heals the brokenhearted and binds up their wounds."* Healing may be painful, but it leads to wholeness.

3. **Trust in the Refining Power of the Wait:** Know that God is using this time to shape you, preparing you to receive His promises fully. **James 1:3-4 (NIV)** reminds us, *"the testing of your faith produces perseverance. Let perseverance finish its work so that you may be mature and complete, not lacking anything."*

4. **Embrace Intimacy with Jesus in the Process:** Use this time to deepen your relationship with Jesus. As you draw near to Him, you'll find comfort, strength, and joy in His presence, even as you wait. **Psalm 73:28 (NIV)** encourages us, *"But as for me, it is good to be near God. I have made the Sovereign LORD my refuge".*

5. **Focus on His Purpose in the Process:** Remember that the waiting isn't just about the promise—it's also about the transformation. Trust that He is equipping you for your future and strengthening you for the purpose He has set before you.

Hope deferred is not hope denied. In the waiting, God builds us, refines us, and prepares us for the blessings He has in store for us. Just as Abraham and Sarah finally saw God's promise fulfilled, we too can rest assured that He will bring His promises to pass for us. Let this season be one where faith rises, where character is built, and where hope remains alive, knowing that God's timing is always perfect.

A Prayer for Strength and Healing in the Waiting

Lord, I come to You with a heart that has known both hope and heartache. I thank You for Your promises, and I ask for Your help as I wait for them to come to pass. Transform my mind, helping me to see beyond my circumstances and to trust in Your faithfulness. Heal my heart, Lord, and the hearts of my children, and draw us into deeper intimacy with You. Thank You for using this season to prepare us, to purify us, and to make us whole. May we continue to grow in Your love, knowing that You are with us every step of the way. In Jesus' name, Amen.

Chapter Five

RISING ABOVE APATHY – REIGNITING PASSION

In today's world, it's easy to pursue success, to chase after the image of a "perfect life"—one filled with material comfort, financial stability, and everything we think will bring us happiness. But sometimes, even when we have everything we thought we wanted, a gnawing emptiness remains, pulling us back to something deeper, something more fulfilling. True passion for life, real purpose, and lasting joy can only be found in a relationship with Jesus.

The Bible reminds us of the importance of keeping our passion for God alive. **Revelation 3:15-16 (NIV)** warns, *"I know your deeds, that you are neither cold nor hot... So, because you are lukewarm—neither hot nor cold—I am about to spit you out of my mouth."* God desires that we approach Him with a wholehearted love, a fresh passion that keeps our hearts alive and vibrant in His presence. When our hearts burn for Him, we experience a new life that goes beyond temporary happiness, reaching the true fulfillment He desires for us.

Empty Success to True Fulfillment: The Story of King Solomon

King Solomon, the son of David, was renowned for his wisdom, wealth, and achievements. He had everything the world could offer: unmatched wealth, vast influence, and the respect of other nations. God blessed Solomon abundantly, and he built a magnificent temple in Jerusalem, filling it with beautiful treasures. Solomon achieved a level of success and prosperity that few could imagine.

Yet, despite all of his wealth, accomplishments, and wisdom, Solomon eventually realized that these things could not bring him true fulfillment. In the Book of Ecclesiastes, he reflects on this emptiness, saying, *"I have seen all the things that are done under the sun; all of them are meaningless, a chasing after the wind"* **Ecclesiastes 1:14 (NIV)**. He observed that his achievements, apart from God, left him unfulfilled and restless.

Through his journey, Solomon learned a powerful lesson: that nothing in this world—no amount of wealth, pleasure, or achievement—can replace a meaningful relationship with God. At the end of the Book of Ecclesiastes, he shares a profound truth: *"Fear God and keep his commandments, for this is the duty of all mankind"* **Ecclesiastes 12:13 (NIV)**. Solomon came to understand that true fulfillment is found in seeking God first and aligning one's life with His will, not in accumulating worldly successes.

Solomon's story serves as a powerful reminder of the biblical principle found within **Matthew 6:33 (NIV)**: *"But seek first his kingdom and his righteousness, and all these things will be given to you as well."* Despite his early pursuit of wealth and success, Solomon ultimately discovered that only a life centered on God could satisfy the soul's deepest longings. His journey from empty success to true fulfillment invites us to examine our own lives and to prioritize our relationship with God as the foundation of lasting joy and purpose within our lives.

My Story: When Success Isn't Enough

There was a time in my life when, by all outward appearances, I seemed to "have it all." I had the home, the financial security, the healthy children, and the freedom to do as I pleased. I could shop, travel, and indulge in the luxuries of life whenever I wanted. But beneath that picture-perfect life, my marriage was in turmoil. We had everything that should have brought happiness, yet something was missing. The struggles in my marriage continued to build, filling our home with tension, distance, and unresolved pain.

One night, after a particularly difficult fight with my now ex-husband, I reached my breaking point. The weight of it all was too much to bear, and in desperation I turned to the only place I hadn't yet looked—God. With tears streaming down my face, I cried out to Him, pleading for help. To my surprise, He responded. I felt a pull towards Him, a deep longing to know Him in a way I never had before.

This response shocked me because, for a very long time I had known about God—I had heard His name, gone through the motions, and believed in His existence. But I had never experienced a relationship where I truly knew Him. I didn't know Him as a faithful Father, as someone who cared deeply about my pain and had the power to lead me through it.

As I leaned into Jesus, seeking to build a relationship with Him, I noticed something unexpected: the closer I drew to Him, the more my marriage seemed to unravel. It was as if the two realities couldn't coexist. The peace I was finding in Jesus began to reveal the deep fractures in my marital relationship, and it felt like I was trying to mix oil and water. The more I pursued the wholeness and hope that Jesus offered, the more the brokenness in my marriage became undeniable.

At the time, I didn't fully understand why things were falling apart, but as I continued to seek God, I realized that my struggles weren't just with my husband or myself. I was facing a battle far beyond the physical realm. As **Ephesians 6:12 (NIV)** says, *"For our* *struggle is not against flesh and blood, but against the rulers, against the authorities, against the powers of this dark world and against the spiritual forces of evil in the heavenly realms."* My marriage was under relentless attack, and the enemy exploited every unhealed wound and unresolved trauma between us, using them as weapons to sow division, pain, and chaos in an effort to tear our family apart.

Through this journey, God opened my eyes to see that we both needed healing—not just for our marriage and family but also for ourselves. We had wounds, scars, and unaddressed trauma that had surfaced in our relationship. These were things I had pushed aside for years, and had even forgotten about, but God was now bringing them to light. Though my marriage ultimately didn't survive, I emerged with a fresh passion and purpose rooted in God. Through the pain, God taught me that true fulfillment doesn't come from outward success but from the deep and lasting relationship we have with Him.

True fulfillment doesn't come from what we accumulate or achieve in this world, but from aligning our lives with God's purpose and seeking His kingdom above all else.

In a world that often equates success with wealth, status, or possessions, Jesus reminds us that these things are temporary and can never satisfy our deepest needs. Instead, when we prioritize our relationship with God—seeking Him first and aligning our lives with His will—everything else falls into place. This kind of fulfillment goes beyond what material success can bring us temporarily. Filling our hearts with peace, joy, and purpose can only come from a life rooted in God's love.

To move from empty success to true fulfillment, we're invited to redefine what success truly means. God's definition of success isn't about external achievements but about a life that reflects His love, serves His purpose, and impacts others. This principle reminds us that when we make God our foundation, we find a fulfillment that cannot be shaken by life's circumstances.

God's definition of success isn't about external achievements but about a life that reflects His love, serves His purpose, and impacts others.

Biblical Principles to Reignite Passion for God and Life

1. **Pursue Wholehearted Surrender:** Sometimes, true passion for God begins when we surrender our preconceived ideas of what life should look like. Give Him your plans, dreams, and heartaches. As **Psalm 37:4 (ESV)** says, *"Delight yourself in the LORD, and he will give you the desires of your heart."* Let your heart's desire be Him above all else.

2. **Recognize the Spiritual Battles Around You:** Not every struggle is rooted in the physical. Just as I learned, our true battles are often spiritual. Equip yourself with God's armor through prayer, scripture and faith, trusting that He will stand with you in every struggle. **Ephesians 6:11 (NIV)** encourages us to *"Put on the full armor of God, so that you can take your stand against the devil's schemes."*

3. **Allow God to Heal Old Wounds:** Sometimes, the lack of passion in our lives stems from unhealed trauma and unresolved pain. Open your heart to God's healing, allowing

Him to restore the parts of you that have been broken. **Psalm 147:3 (NIV)** promises, *"He heals the brokenhearted and binds up their wounds."* Healing paves the way for renewed passion within our lives.

4. **Seek Intimacy with Jesus Daily:** Passion for God grows in the quiet moments of prayer, worship, and time spent in His presence. The closer you draw to Him, the more alive your heart becomes. As **James 4:8 (NIV)** says, *"Come near to God and he will come near to you."* Let your daily walk with Him fuel your passion.

5. **Redefine Success through God's Eyes:** True success is not defined by material possessions or social status. It's found in a life aligned with God's purpose, one that impacts others with His love. **Matthew 6:33 (NIV)** teaches, *"seek first his kingdom and his righteousness, and all these things will be given to you as well."* Allow God's purpose to redefine what "having it all" truly means.

A vibrant relationship with God is the foundation for a life filled with passion and purpose. As you seek Him daily, as you heal and grow, you'll find a joy that goes beyond outward success. Like a spark that lights a fire, your pursuit of Jesus will reignite your heart, bringing renewed excitement and a deeper purpose to every area of your life. Let your passion for Him be the driving force behind all you do, knowing that true fulfillment is found in His love, His peace, and His promises.

A Prayer for Renewed Passion and Purpose

Lord, I come before You, acknowledging that my heart often drifts toward the things of this world. I ask that You rekindle a passion within me that burns solely for You. Teach me to delight in Your presence, to see my struggles through Your eyes, and to live with a purpose that goes beyond my own desires. Heal the wounds that have kept me distant and draw me closer to You each day. Let my life be a reflection of Your love, a testimony of true fulfillment found in You alone. In Jesus' name, Amen.

Chapter Six

FINDING PEACE IN THE OVERWHELM – RESTING IN GOD'S PRESENCE

Life often overwhelms us. The weight of responsibilities, the pressure to keep moving forward, and the constant noise of our own thoughts can sometimes feel like a storm swirling around us. In those moments, we search for peace, for a place of calm where we can breathe freely again. But the peace we're seeking isn't something we can achieve on our own. It's a gift from God—a peace that surpasses all understanding **Philippians 4:7**, a peace that fills the spaces of our hearts that feel frayed and torn.

Jesus speaks of this peace in **John 14:27 (NIV)**, saying, *"Peace I leave with you; my peace I give you. I do not give to you as the world gives. Do not let your hearts be troubled and do not be afraid."* His peace isn't like the temporary comfort we find in the world; it's a divine calm that settles our hearts, even in the most overwhelming times. When we turn to God in the midst of our storms, we find a refuge, a sanctuary where His presence soothes our fears and reminds us that we're not alone.

A Story of Finding Peace in God's Presence: Jesus Calms the Storm

One of the most comforting stories in the Bible is that of Jesus calming the storm. After a long day of teaching, Jesus and His disciples set out to cross the Sea of Galilee. As they were sailing, a violent storm arose, and waves crashed into the boat. The disciples, terrified, woke Jesus, crying out, *"Lord, save us! We're going to drown!"* **Matthew 8:25(NIV)**.

But Jesus, calm and undisturbed, rebuked the winds and waves, saying, *"Quiet! Be still!"* **Mark 4:39 (NIV)**. Immediately, the sea was calm, and a deep peace fell over the waters. The disciples were amazed, asking each other, *"Who is this? Even the winds and the waves obey him!"* **Mark 4:41 (NIV)**.

In that moment, Jesus demonstrated the power of His presence to bring peace. The storm was real, the fear was real, but so was Jesus' authority over it. This story is a reminder that, even when life feels out of control, when we're overwhelmed and frightened, we can find peace by turning to Him. He is with us in every storm, calming the chaos around us and within us.

My Journey to Find Peace in the Overwhelm

Let me tell you, I never thought I'd be the person to have an anxiety attack. I mean, I've handled a lot—kids, work, life's curveballs—no problem, right? But there I was, in what felt like a scene from a movie, convinced I was dying. Yes, dying. My heart was racing, my breath was shallow, and I thought, *'This is it. I'm about to go meet Jesus, right here in my living room.'*

So, what did I do? I called my friend. Now, let me paint you a picture of this friend: she is the busiest person I know, someone who would usually need a few days' notice to pencil me in. However, that day, she picked up immediately and, like a superhero, raced to my side. She didn't have a clue as to how to handle a full-on, dramatic anxiety attack—who does, really?—so she just sat next to me, and she started praying. However, it didn't quite relieve the anxiety. Then she did the only other thing she could think of—she opened her Bible and started reading it to me.

You know what? It worked. God's Word wrapped around me like a warm embrace, washing over my fear and quieting the chaos deep within me. In that moment, it was as if God Himself whispered to my heart, *"Hey, I've got you."* A peace I can't fully explain settled over me, not because my circumstances had changed, but because His presence reminded me that my spirit was secure in Him, no matter what my body was feeling.

As I write this, tears well up in my eyes at the thought of how powerful His Word is and how deeply He loves us. His love isn't fleeting or conditional—it's steady, constant, and strong enough to meet us in our darkest moments. Oh, what a sweet and tender reminder that His promises never fail. If He could carry me through that storm, I know He can do the same for you. Let this be a reminder: God sees you, He hears your cries, and His love is holding you, even now.

His love isn't fleeting or conditional—it's steady, constant, and strong enough to meet us in our darkest moments.

I wish I could say the anxiety attacks stopped there, but they didn't. They seemed to pop up anytime they felt like it, sometimes even as I was just sitting with my boys, trying tame my mind by watching TV. Out of nowhere, boom—another anxiety attack. It was like having an unwanted guest show up unannounced, over and over again. I started to run to my prayer closet every time anxiety came knocking, to take it all to God.

You know what? God met me there. Every. Single. Time. I can't explain it, but as soon as I closed that prayer closet door, the anxiety would fade, and a peace beyond words would take over. That closet became my secret weapon, my own little fortress of solitude. It was like God's personal invitation, saying, *"Come on in, let's talk about it."*

Now here's where it gets funny. My boys started to catch on. They'd see me go in there and come out calm and collected, so they knew something special happened in that closet. One day, my youngest got into a bit of trouble in the kitchen—flour everywhere, you name it. When I came out of the prayer closet and saw him looking like a mini baker gone wild, he looked at me, sheepishly, and said, *"Momma, it's okay, just go to the prayer closet!"* He knew where to send me when things got messy!

That closet isn't just a place anymore; it's a reminder that God is always ready to meet us. Whether we're full of joy or filled with worry, He's there, waiting with open arms, saying, *"Come on in, and leave your worries here."* I learned that the peace I needed was always within reach, not because of my own strength, but because of His presence. So, if you ever find yourself overwhelmed, find a little space—a quiet room, a cozy chair, even a closet—and go meet with Him. Let Him fill you with peace that only He can give.

Biblical Principles for Finding Peace in the Overwhelm

1. **Run to God First:** When anxiety and overwhelm threaten to overtake you, let God be the first place you go. In **Psalm 91:1-2 (NIV)**, we read, *"Whoever dwells in the shelter of the Most High will rest in the shadow of the Almighty. I will say of the LORD, 'He is my refuge and my fortress, my God, in whom I trust.'"* Find your refuge in Him, trusting that He is your shelter in the storm.

2. **Invite God's Peace Through Prayer:** Prayer is a powerful tool to quiet our hearts. **Philippians 4:6-7 (NIV)** encourages us, *"Do not be anxious about anything, but in every situation, by prayer and petition, with thanksgiving, present your requests to God. And the peace of God, which transcends all understanding, will guard your hearts and your minds in Christ Jesus."* Pour out your worries to God, and let His peace guard you.

3. **Meditate on God's Word:** Just as my friend read Scripture to me during my anxiety attack, God's Word has the power to calm our hearts. In **Psalm 119:165 (NIV)**, we're reminded, *"Great peace have those who love your law, and nothing can make them stumble."* When anxiety arises, immerse yourself in His Word, letting it bring peace to your soul.

4. **Create a Place of Meeting with God:** Whether it's a closet, a corner, or a chair, create a space where you can meet with God. **Matthew 6:6 (NIV)** says, *"But when you pray, go into your room, close the door and pray to your Father, who is unseen. Then your Father, who sees what is done in secret, will reward you."* Make this place your sanctuary, a place where His presence brings rest.

5. **Trust in Jesus' Authority Over the Storm:** Remember that Jesus has the power to calm every storm. Just as He calmed the sea for the disciples, He can calm the anxieties within you. **Mark 4:39** reminds us that He can speak peace into any situation. Trust in His authority, knowing He is with you always.

No matter what overwhelms you, know that God's presence is a place of peace. Just as He calmed the sea for the disciples and met me in my prayer closet, He will meet you wherever you call on Him. In Him, you'll find rest, comfort, and a peace that the world cannot take away.

Let His presence become your sanctuary, your shelter in the storm, and your refuge every day.

A Prayer for Peace in the Overwhelm

Father, I come to You in the midst of my anxieties and fears, seeking Your peace that surpasses understanding. Thank You for being my refuge, my safe haven. Teach me to run to You first, to find comfort in Your presence, and to rest in Your promises. Help me to release every worry to You, trusting that You hold me in the palm of Your hand. Thank You for meeting me in my storm and for calming my heart with Your love. In Jesus' name, Amen.

Chapter Seven

HEALING THE HEART – OVERCOMING SADNESS AND EMPTINESS

Sadness and emptiness can feel like unwelcome guests that linger in the quiet moments of our lives, sometimes settling into our hearts so subtly that we barely recognize them. But God, in His love, invites us to experience healing and fullness in place of that sadness, joy in place of our emptiness. He knows the hidden wounds, the unspoken longings, and the secret sorrows we carry—and He is always ready to bring us to a place of peace and wholeness.

The Bible reminds us of God's tender care in **Psalm 34:18 (NIV):** *"The Lord is close to the brokenhearted and saves those who are crushed in spirit."* God doesn't look at our sadness or emptiness as burdens; instead, He sees them as an invitation to draw closer to us, to heal what has been broken, and to restore what we may have lost.

A Story of God's Healing Love: Hannah's Prayer

One of the most beautiful stories of God's healing in the Bible is the story of Hannah, a woman who knew the ache of sadness and emptiness. Hannah longed to have a child, but year after year, her prayers seemed to go unanswered. The weight of her sorrow was so heavy that she would weep and pray in deep anguish, feeling empty and alone.

One day, as she poured out her heart in prayer at the temple, she made a vow to God, promising that if He blessed her with a son, she would dedicate him back to the Lord. The priest, Eli, noticed her praying and, after understanding her grief, blessed her. After that encounter, Hannah's heart shifted. She got up, *"and her face was no longer downcast"* **1 Samuel 1:18 (NIV)**. Although her circumstances hadn't yet changed, her heart had found peace. God eventually blessed her with a son, Samuel, and her joy overflowed as she praised the Lord for His faithfulness.

Hannah's story shows us that healing often begins not when our circumstances change, but when we bring our deepest pain to God. When we pour out our hearts to Him, He meets us, fills us with peace, and reminds us that He is with us in every season of waiting, sadness, and emptiness. God didn't just give Hannah a son; He gave her heart healing and joy that went beyond her desires.

My Journey to Find Joy and Overcome Sadness and Emptiness

Looking back, I can see how God's hand was guiding me through a journey of healing, though I was unaware of that deep need hidden within my heart. Growing up, I had a wonderful mother and father who provided for me and cared for me, yet there was one thing I never heard from them: "I love you." My parents loved me in their way, but somehow, those three little words were never spoken to me. As a child, I didn't notice it; it was just how things were. But as I got older, a quiet ache began to grow—a longing I didn't fully understand or know how to address.

Without realizing it, I began seeking out those words from other people. I found myself drawn to anyone who would say, *"I love you."* I didn't understand why those words held such power over me, only that they filled a gap, soothing an emptiness that I couldn't explain.

This didn't mean that these people always knew what real love was, or that their words came with genuine caring for me. Often, they didn't. But hearing *"I love you"* felt like a balm to my heart, and I let myself be drawn into relationships I probably should have run from.

These relationships, though they spoke the words I craved, often left me with a even deeper sense of emptiness. They weren't built on the solid foundation of real love, and the void in my heart only grew. Yet, through all of this, Jesus was patiently waiting, ready to reveal what true love looks like. I didn't realize it then, but He was preparing me for a healing journey that would transform my life.

As I grew closer to Jesus, I began to surrender my heart to Him bit by bit. Every day, I would lay my burdens at His feet—my worries, my sadness, my longing to feel loved. It became a process of daily surrender, a walk of faith that required me to trust Him with all the broken pieces of my heart. As I did this, He began to show me the root of my sadness, revealing to me that it was rooted in the words I never heard as a child. He gently brought those memories to the surface, not to harm me, but to heal me.

Each day, as I placed my heart in His hands, I experienced something unexpected: joy. I didn't know it at the time, but a healing process was unfolding with every step of faith I took. Jesus was showing me that the love I had been searching for couldn't be filled by empty words or fleeting relationships; it could only be filled by Him. His love became my joy, lifting the darkness and filling the void that had lingered for so long in my life and in my heart.

Here's what I want you to know: Jesus longs to heal your heart, too. Whatever sadness, pain, or trauma you carry, He already knows and He's ready to bring it to the surface—not to harm you but to heal you. There are some wounds that only He can touch, some hurts that no medicine, no therapist, and no worldly remedy can fully address. He sees the very roots of your pain, even the parts that you may not fully understand yourself yet, and He longs to heal them even more than you want to be healed.

He sees the very roots of your pain, even the parts that you may not fully understand yourself yet, and He longs to heal them even more than you want to be healed.

When we surrender our hearts to Jesus, He gently reveals what's hidden, not to break us but to restore us. He is the only one who can reach into the deepest places, bringing light into the darkness and joy in place of emptiness. Just as He filled my heart with joy through His love, He is ready to do the same for you. He's not waiting for you to be perfect or to have it all figured out—He's simply waiting for you to say, *"Jesus, I need You."*

His love is real, and it's personal. It's the love that fills every gap, that brings healing to the most broken of places, and it reminds us that we are never alone. Jesus wants to walk this journey with you, to bring you into a place of peace, joy, and wholeness that only He can provide. I may not have heard *"I love you"* from my parents, but I hear it every day from Him. He whispers it in the quiet moments, declares it to me through His Word, and proves it through His constant presence. Let Him heal your heart too, and fill it with a joy that overflows.

Biblical Principles for Overcoming Sadness and Emptiness

1. **Bring Your Pain to God:** Healing begins when we, like Hannah, pour out our hearts before God, sharing even the sadness and emptiness we may not fully understand. **Psalm 62:8 (NIV)** reminds us to, *"Trust in him at all times, you people; pour out your hearts to him, for God is our refuge."*

2. **Receive God's Love Daily:** Sometimes, our hearts need to be reminded that we are loved deeply by God. **Romans 5:8 (NIV)** tells us, *"But God demonstrates his own love for us in this: While we were still sinners, Christ died for us."* Allow His love to be the foundation of your healing.

3. **Trust That God Reveals to Heal:** God doesn't reveal our hurts to leave us broken; He reveals them so that He can heal them. Let Him show you the hidden areas that need healing, knowing that His desire is to bring you into wholeness.

4. **Surrender Your Worries and Wounds:** Healing is a process, and it often requires daily surrender. As you give your worries and wounds to God, trust that He is doing a work in you. **1 Peter 5:7 (NIV)** encourages us to: *"Cast all your anxiety on him because he cares for you."*

5. **Find Joy in His Presence:** In His presence, we find fullness of joy, a joy that goes beyond our circumstances. **Psalm 16:11 (NIV)** says, *"You make known to me the path of life; you will fill me with joy in your presence, with eternal pleasures at your right hand."*

God is the ultimate healer of hearts, and He longs to bring you into a place of joy, wholeness, and peace. Like Hannah, bring your hurts and your heart to Him, trusting that He sees every tear and hears every prayer. Know that even in the quiet moments, when you feel empty or sad, He is working in you, drawing you closer, and filling you with a joy that only He can give. Let each day with Him be a step in your healing journey, knowing that He is with you every step of the way.

A Prayer for Healing and Joy

Lord, I come to You with a heart that has known sadness and emptiness. Thank You for being my healer, my comfort, and my source of joy. Reveal the areas in my heart that need Your touch, and help me to surrender every burden to You. Teach me to find joy in Your presence, and fill me with the peace that only You can give. Thank You for Your love that restores, heals, and fills my heart with hope. In Jesus' name, Amen.

Chapter Eight

EMBRACING WORTHINESS – SEEING OURSELVES THROUGH GOD'S EYES

In a world that constantly tells us who we should be, it's easy to forget who we already are in Christ. So many voices try to define us—our past mistakes, others' opinions, even our own fears and insecurities. But God has spoken the final word on who we are, and His word is the only one that truly matters. We are loved, chosen, redeemed, and new creations in Christ Jesus.

Imagine this: You are a child of the King! **1 Peter 2:9 (NIV)** declares: *"But you are a chosen people, a royal priesthood, a holy nation, God's special possession, that you may declare the praises of him who called you out of darkness into his wonderful light."* You were created with purpose, and your life is precious to God. You're not defined by your struggles, your failures, or what others say. Your identity is secure in Him, and because of that, you are entitled to all the riches of Heaven. You are co-heirs with Christ, and nothing can separate you from His love **Romans 8:35-39.**

When we fully embrace this identity, we begin to see ourselves as God sees us. We are empowered to walk in confidence, knowing that we are cherished beyond measure. Every promise, every blessing, every bit of love and grace in Heaven is ours because we belong to Him. When we see ourselves this way, we're no longer bound by the labels or limitations that the world tries to place upon us; we are free to be who God created us to be.

Peter's Journey to Embracing His Identity in Christ

What about Peter? His journey to discovering who he was in Christ is one of the most powerful examples in the Bible. After denying Jesus three times out of fear and shame **Luke 22:54-62**, Peter felt broken, unworthy, and unsure of his purpose. In his discouragement, he returned to what he knew—fishing **John 21:3**. It was as if he had cast aside the identity Jesus had spoken over him, feeling unfit to carry the mantle of being a "fisher of men" **Matthew 4:19**.

But then, in the midst of his ordinary routine, something extraordinary happened. Jesus appeared on the shore, calling out to the disciples and performing a miracle similar to the one Peter had witnessed when he first followed Him **John 21:4-6**. When John recognized the Lord and said, *"It is the Lord!"* **John 21:7**, Peter's reaction was immediate and bold. He put on his outer garment, a symbolic act of reclaiming his identity, as he jumped into the water, swimming to shore without hesitation.

In that moment, Peter wasn't just running to Jesus; he was stepping back into who he was called to be. Jesus, in His grace, didn't meet Peter with condemnation for his denial but with reconciliation and restoration. One evening around a fire, the same setting where Peter had denied Him, Jesus asked Peter three times, *"Do you love me?"* **John 21:15-17**. Each response was an opportunity to counteract Peter's denial, restoring him fully to the mission Jesus had for him.

This story is a reminder that no failure, shame, or fear can cancel the purpose God has for your life. Just like Peter, you may feel like you've fallen short, but Jesus is always ready to meet you with grace, to remind you of who you truly are, and to call you forward into your purpose. If Peter could go from denying Christ to becoming the rock upon which the church was built **Matthew 16:18**, imagine what God can do with your life when you embrace who He says you are. Step out, put on your "outer garment," and run to the One who restores, redeems, and equips you for the purpose only you can fulfill.

My Journey to Discover Who I Am in Christ

For a long time, I wrestled with the question, "Who am I, really?" Life had handed me enough curveballs—challenges, painful experiences, and, yes, even a messy divorce—to make me feel like my identity was in shambles. I thought I had it figured out at one point: I was the accomplished engineer with a bachelor's degree, the go-getter with an associate's degree, the devoted mom, the supportive wife… and let's not forget, the perfect party planner. It was like collecting titles for a résumé I didn't even want. Here's the thing: when life took those titles and shook them up, I was left staring at the pieces, wondering who I really was.

If you've ever felt like your identity is tied to what you do or the roles you play, let me encourage you—it's not. Those things might describe you, but they don't *define* you. I didn't know it then, but God was about to show me that my true identity wasn't in what I had achieved, endured, or even lost. It was in something far greater: who He says I am. Let me tell you, when God starts telling you who you are, it changes everything.

God, in His infinite kindness, has an extraordinary way of showing us who we truly are—usually when we least expect it and often in ways that make us say, *"Oh, You were serious about that, Lord?"* He began revealing pieces of my identity to me through dreams, visions, His Word, and even prophecies. Each time, there was an undeniable knowing in my heart that these weren't just random thoughts—they were from Him. Through these revelations, I began to see myself through His eyes. I wasn't just someone trying to survive life's trials; I was His beloved, His chosen and treasured child, called to a unique purpose in His Kingdom. Talk about a perspective shift!

As I leaned into His truth, God began to connect the dots in a way only He can. The challenges I had faced—the heartbreaks, the struggles, the moments when I thought I couldn't go on—weren't wasted. Instead, they were the training ground for something far greater. I realized that the areas where I had felt the most defeated were the very places He was now calling me to bring light for others. The struggles I had once begged Him to remove were now the testimony He was using to equip me to help others. Isn't that just like God? He takes what feels like ashes and turns it into something beautiful **Isaiah 61:3**.

This journey of discovering who I am in Christ has been nothing short of liberating. To know that my identity isn't tied to what I've done, what I've failed at, or what others think of me, but rather to the unshakable truth of who I am in Him, has changed everything. I am deeply loved, purposefully chosen, and fully equipped for the life He has called me to live. Knowing this has given me the courage to step boldly into the future, not with all the answers, but with full confidence in the One who holds them.

Dear reader, here's the thing: God wants you to know who you are in Him, too. You are not defined by your mistakes, the limitations others have placed on you, or even the struggles you're wrestling with today. You are His beloved, His masterpiece, and He has a unique and beautiful purpose for your life. Those challenges that feel like they're trying to take you out? They're not random; they're indicators of how

God plans to use you. The very places where you feel stretched thin are the places where He's equipping you to become a light for others.

The very places where you feel stretched thin are the places where He's equipping you to become a light for others.

Here's a little secret: God doesn't waste *anything*. Not a single tear, heartbreak, or "Why me?" moment is left unused. **Romans 8:28 (NIV)** says, *"And we know that in all things God works for the good of those who love Him, who have been called according to His purpose."* This means your mess is His masterpiece in the making. Every trial, every lesson, every long season of waiting—it's all being woven into His perfect plan for you.

God wants you to know that in Christ, you are made new and entitled to the riches of Heaven—not because of anything you've done, but because of who you are to Him. When you begin to see yourself through His eyes, you'll discover a strength, hope, and purpose that will blow your mind. You'll laugh at what once made you cry and stand firm where you once felt shaken.

So, as you navigate this crazy, beautiful, and sometimes messy thing called life, hold on to this truth: God is using *all of it*. Every setback, every heartbreak, and every tiny victory is leading you closer to Him and preparing you for the incredible things He has in store for you. Let this knowledge fill you with a renewed hope and courage to keep moving forward. You are deeply loved, fully known, and perfectly purposed by the Creator of the universe. Trust me, He's just getting started with you.

Biblical Principles to Embrace Your Identity in Christ

1. **Remember You Are Chosen and Loved:** God chose you long before you could ever choose Him. In **Ephesians 1:4-5 (NIV)**, we read, *"For he chose us in him before the creation of the world to be holy and blameless in his sight."* He calls you His beloved, and nothing you could ever do would change His love for you.

2. **Claim Your Identity as a New Creation:** In Christ, you are made new. **2 Corinthians 5:17 (NIV)** promises, *"Therefore, if anyone is in Christ, the new creation has come: The old has gone, the new is here!"* Let go of the old labels, the past hurts, and embrace the new identity God has given you.

3. **See Yourself as Co-Heir with Christ:** God has given you the same inheritance as His Son. **Romans 8:17 (NIV)** reminds us, *"Now if we are children, then we are heirs—heirs of God and co-heirs with Christ."* Every promise and blessing in Heaven is yours through Jesus.

4. **Walk Boldly in Your Purpose:** The struggles you've faced are often a sign of where God will use you to make the greatest impact. Trust that He has equipped you for a purpose beyond yourself. **Jeremiah 29:11 (NIV)** declares, *"'For I know the plans I have for you,' declares the LORD, 'plans to prosper you and not to harm you, plans to give you hope and a future'."*

5. **Let God Define You, Not the World:** The world may try to label you, but God's word is the final authority concerning who you are. **Galatians 2:20 (NIV)** reminds us, *"I have been crucified with Christ and I no longer live, but Christ lives in me."* Your

identity is hidden in Him, free from any limitations or labels the world tries to place upon you.

Embracing your identity in Christ isn't a once-and-done kind of thing—it's a daily choice to see yourself through His eyes instead of the distorted lens the world often hands us. Let's be real: some days, that's easier said than done. Here's the truth that doesn't change: you are loved, chosen, and called with a purpose that's bigger than you can even imagine.

Walk boldly in this truth, even on the days when you feel like you're just trying to survive your to-do list or wondering if God really knows what He's doing. Every promise of Heaven is yours, every word He has spoken over you is true, and every blessing in His Kingdom is for you. Your identity isn't based upon what you've done or how you feel—it's rooted in what He's already declared about you.

As you live in this confidence, remember that those struggles you've been through- they're not just there to make life hard. God uses every experience as a tool to impact others, to bring hope, and to reveal His love to a world desperate for it. So, let go of what the world says about you—you are far more than the titles, failures, or even successes other people see. You are a child of the King, handcrafted for greatness. Embrace it, live it, and let His love shine so brightly through you that others can't help but see Him too.

A Prayer for Embracing Your Identity

Lord, thank You for calling me Your child, for choosing me, and for loving me beyond measure. Help me to see myself as You see me, and to let go of any labels or lies that don't align with Your truth. Remind me daily that I am Your beloved, a new creation, and a co-heir with Christ. Show me how to walk boldly in my purpose, knowing that You have equipped me for every good work. May I live my life grounded in the identity You have given me, reflecting Your love and grace in everything I do. In Jesus' name, Amen.

Chapter Nine

BREAKING FREE FROM POWERLESSNESS – WALKING IN GOD'S AUTHORITY

Imagine walking through each day knowing that no matter what you face, the power within you is greater than anything this world can throw at you. As children of God, this isn't just wishful thinking—it's a reality. The same Spirit that raised Jesus from the dead lives in us **Romans 8:11**, empowering us to face challenges with strength and assurance. **1 John 4:4 (KJV)** reminds us, *"Greater is He that is in you than he that is in the world."* This isn't merely a suggestion; it's a bold declaration of our authority in Christ.

To live with this boldness and authority requires a renewing of the mind. It's a daily process of replacing lies with the truth of God's Word, recognizing that you carry a power that's stronger than anything in this world. Jesus has given us authority to overcome, to stand firm, and to walk in freedom. When we fully grasp this truth, we can boldly stand against any obstacle, knowing that our identity and strength are rooted in Him.

Joshua's story is an inspiring example of someone who embraced God's authority to lead His people into their promised inheritance. After Moses' death, Joshua was tasked with a monumental mission: to lead the Israelites into the land God had promised them. It was no small task. The land was filled with fortified cities and powerful enemies, and Joshua was stepping into a role that had been held by one of the greatest leaders in history. Yet, God's authority over Joshua's life made all the difference.

God's first words to Joshua after Moses' passing were both a charge and a promise: *"Be strong and courageous, because you will lead these people to inherit the land I swore to their ancestors to give them"* **Joshua 1:6 (NIV)**. God reassured Joshua repeatedly, saying, *"As I was with Moses, so I will be with you; I will never leave you nor forsake you"* **Joshua 1:5 (NIV)**. These words weren't just comforting; they were empowering. Joshua wasn't stepping into this role on his own authority, he was walking under God's command and provision.

One of Joshua's most remarkable demonstrations of authority came during the battle of Jericho. God gave him specific instructions that didn't make logical sense: *march around the city once a day for six days, then seven times on the seventh day, and blow trumpets* **Joshua 6:2-5 (NIV)**. To a human mind, this might have seemed ridiculous—walls don't fall because of marching and trumpet blasts. But Joshua obeyed, fully trusting in God's authority over the battle.

The result? The walls of Jericho collapsed, and the Israelites claimed their first victory in the Promised Land **Joshua 6:20**. This miraculous event wasn't just a demonstration of God's power, it was a confirmation of what happens when we step into His authority, obey His Word, and trust His promises.

Joshua's story reminds us that God's authority is always tied to His promises. When He calls us to step into something new, whether it's a challenge, a calling, or a battle, it's not our strength or strategy that secures the victory, it's His power working through us.

If you're facing something that feels impossible, remember what God said to Joshua: *"Have I not commanded you? Be strong and courageous. Do not be afraid; do not be discouraged, for the Lord your God will be with you wherever you go"* **Joshua 1:9 (NIV)**. Those words aren't just for Joshua—they're for you too.

God's authority equips you to step boldly into His promises. Even when the path doesn't make sense or the battle feels too big, His power is greater than any obstacle. Trust Him, obey His leading, and watch as He does what only He can do. With God, you can walk in the confidence that every step you take is guided by His authority and His unwavering faithfulness.

My Journey to Embracing God's Authority

Let me tell you, for the longest time I didn't quite understand the authority God had given me. Sure, I'd heard sermons about standing firm, but the idea of having any real power against life's challenges seemed... well, a bit out of reach. I was just trying to get through the day without getting knocked over by the latest wave of chaos. However, God had other plans.

My wake-up call came through what seemed like endless attempts on my life—no, seriously! There I was, on my stairmaster, exercising while just minding my own business, trying to get some exercise out of the way, when suddenly the band on the stairmaster broke. Now, if you've ever been on a stairmaster, you know that's a recipe for disaster. I could have had a fall that might have ended my life or at least left me with some serious injuries. Yet somehow, by what I now know was divine protection, I walked away without a scratch.

Then there was the car accident, one of those scenes that should have ended badly. Yet again, I came out of it without a single bruise or bump. At first, I just brushed it off as luck. But after enough of these "close calls," I started to realize this wasn't luck—this was God showing me that His protection was real. I began to see that there was something greater at work, although I was being protected, I was also caught in a cycle, one that needed to be broken.

As I leaned into Scripture, I began to learn about God's authority and this revelation was a game changer. I saw examples of people like Moses, who stood before Pharaoh with nothing but a shepherd's staff and God's Word. Pharaoh had armies, but Moses had God's authority, and guess who won that battle? How about David, a young shepherd who took down a giant with a stone? David wasn't the strongest guy on the battlefield, but he understood that the true power came from God, not from physical strength or fancy weapons.

These stories lit something on fire deep within me. If David and Moses could walk in authority, so could I. Jesus Himself gave us authority, saying in **Luke 10:19 (NIV)**, *"I have given you authority to trample on snakes and scorpions and to overcome all the power of the enemy."* Now, I'm not planning to go about stomping on actual snakes and scorpions anytime soon, but I started to realize that I also didn't have to live under the weight of fear, oppression, or heaviness anymore.

I took this newfound authority seriously. I began to declare God's promises over my life and my boys. Every curse, every negative word that had ever been spoken over us—I broke it in Jesus' name. Let me tell you, things started to change. It wasn't just a feeling of relief; it was as if a real weight had lifted off of us. That daily oppression and heaviness I had been carrying began to disappear, and I felt peace and strength I hadn't known before.

The best part? This authority isn't just for me; it's for you, too! Remember, God doesn't play favorites. Just as He protected Daniel in the lions' den and gave Esther the courage to stand up to a king, He's given each of us the power to stand firm and live boldly. Jesus said in **Matthew 18:18 (NIV)**, *"Truly I tell you, whatever you bind on earth will be bound in heaven, and whatever you loose on earth will be loosed in heaven."* Talk about authority! We don't have to live under the weight of fear or passively accept the things that come against us. With God's authority, we can live victoriously.

If you're feeling stuck in a cycle you can't seem to escape from, know this: God has already given you what you need to break free. The enemy wants you to believe you're powerless, but nothing could be further from the truth. You carry within you a power far greater than anything this world can throw your way—because *greater is He that is in you than he that is in the world* **1 John 4:4 (NIV)**.

So, step into the authority that's already yours. Declare His promises boldly, break the chains that have held you back, and walk in the freedom and peace that He has for you. With God, no cycle is unbreakable, and no situation is beyond redemption. You are equipped, empowered, and deeply loved by the One who has already won the victory for you. Now it's time to walk in it!

Biblical Principles for Living Boldly in God's Authority

1. **Renew Your Mind with Truth:** Knowing who you are in Christ means renewing your mind daily with God's Word. **Romans 12:2 (NIV)** reminds us, *"Do not conform to the pattern of this world, but be transformed by the renewing of your mind."* Replace any lies you have believed with the truth of who you are in Him—chosen, powerful, and free.

2. **Declare Your Authority in Christ:** Jesus has given us authority over all the power of the enemy. **Luke 10:19 (NIV)** says, *"I have given you authority to trample on snakes and scorpions and to overcome all the power of the enemy; nothing will harm*

you." Speak God's Word over your life, breaking every curse and standing firm in His promises.

3. **Reject Fear and Walk in Boldness:** Fear is a tactic of the enemy, but God has given us a spirit of power, love, and a sound mind. **2 Timothy 1:7 (NIV)** says, *"For the Spirit God gave us does not make us timid, but gives us power, love, and self-discipline."* Embrace this truth and walk boldly, knowing that God's power is within you.

4. **Stand Firm Against Oppression:** The enemy has no right to oppress or keep you in bondage. **James 4:7 (NIV)** tells us, *"Submit yourselves, then, to God. Resist the devil, and he will flee from you."* Take a stand against any heaviness, speaking freedom over your life through the authority of Jesus.

5. **Know That God's Power Is Greater:** Remember that no matter what comes against you, God's power within you is greater than any force in this world. **Ephesians 3:20 (NIV)** reminds us, *"Now to him who is able to do immeasurably more than all we ask or imagine, according to his power that is at work within us"*. Trust in this power and walk with confidence.

As a child of God, you carry within you a power that is greater than any obstacle, fear, or attack of the enemy. This power isn't just a concept—it's a reality, rooted in the authority you have in Christ. When you renew your mind with His Word, stand firm on His promises, and declare His truth over your life, you become a force to be reckoned with. The same Spirit that raised Jesus from

When you renew your mind with His Word, stand firm on His promises, and declare His truth over your life, you become a force to be reckoned with.

the dead lives in you **Romans 8:11**, empowering you to overcome, to stand strong, and to live in freedom.

Don't settle for a life of oppression, heaviness, or fear. You have been given the authority to walk boldly in your purpose, knowing that God is for you, with you, and within you. So, take hold of this truth, embrace the power He has given you, and live each day in the fullness of His love, joy, and freedom. You are more than a conqueror, you are equipped for every challenge and unstoppable in His strength. Walk in boldness and authority—you are a child of the King.

A Prayer for Boldness and Authority

Lord, I thank You for the authority You have given me as Your child. Help me to renew my mind daily with Your truth, to reject fear, and to walk boldly in the power You have placed within me. I declare that every lie and curse spoken over my life is broken, and I stand firm in the freedom You have given me. Teach me to see myself through Your eyes, to know that greater is He who is in me than anything that could come against me. Thank You for Your protection, Your love, and Your unwavering presence. In Jesus' name, Amen.

Chapter Ten

BREAKING THE CYCLE – FINDING LASTING CHANGE IN CHRIST

Have you ever noticed how some patterns stick to us like glue? For many of us, the struggle with money is a cycle we can't seem to escape. Whether it's worrying about bills, feeling like there's never enough, or striving endlessly to "get ahead," these patterns create a poverty mindset. There's good news: you don't have to live in that cycle forever. God gives us the power to break free and live in true abundance—not the kind defined by bank balances or possessions, but by peace, purpose, and provision that only He can give.

The Bible is packed with stories of people who broke free from their apparent limitations and lived fully in God's abundance. One of my favorites is the story of the Israelites in the wilderness. For years, they had a poverty mindset, doubting that God would provide. Every time they hit a challenge, they wondered if they'd survive, even though God had already parted the Red Sea, led them with a pillar of fire, and provided daily manna. Sound familiar? Like us, they needed to break free from old patterns of doubt and learn to live in trust and confidence in the goodness of God.

Jesus taught us this principle clearly in **Matthew 6:33 (NIV)**: *"But seek first his kingdom and his righteousness, and all these things will be given to you as well."* When we prioritize God, He provides all we need. When we stop chasing the things of this world and focus on Him, we find that our needs are met, often in ways we couldn't have anticipated.

If you've been striving, feeling stuck on the "go-getter" treadmill, or constantly comparing what you have with what you wish you had, take heart. You don't have to live stuck in that cycle. God wants to free you from the poverty mindset and bring you into a place of true abundance—one rooted in His provision and purpose for your life.

True wealth is waking up with a heart full of peace, knowing that you are deeply loved, valuable, and cared for by your Heavenly Father. It's not defined by material gain, but by the richness of a life lived in His love. When we place our trust in God as our provider, we find freedom from the fear of "not having enough." We discover a wealth that goes beyond possessions—a wealth rooted in His endless grace, peace, and purpose. This is the freedom God wants for you, and you can step into it today

My Journey to Break the Poverty Mindset

Growing up, we didn't have much, but we had each other. My family lived in a rough neighborhood, and every now and then, our home would be broken into. The things my father had worked so hard to provide for us were taken, and each time, it felt like a piece of security was stripped away. We were grateful for God's protection, but life was far from easy. We lived paycheck to paycheck, sometimes barely making it through. My father worked hard, yet we always seemed to be just scraping by. One Christmas Eve, we were planning to visit family in Mexico, a tradition we cherished. However, that morning, I woke up to the sound of loud knocking on our front door, followed by the flashes of a flashlight through my bedroom window. My sisters and I got up, confused, only to discover that a sheriff was there to repossess our only vehicle due to missed payments.

That Christmas, we were left with no vehicle, no Christmas tree, and no groceries in the fridge since we'd planned to travel. It was a hard reality check, and I remember feeling that deep ache of "not enough." As I got older, this scarcity mindset followed me. I believed that if I could just have "more," life would feel secure and fulfilling. I didn't realize that for all my working life I was chasing money, and not God. I eventually learned that my belief that there was never enough was part of a poverty mindset—a mindset that holds us in a cycle of always feeling one step behind, always striving, yet never arriving.

In today's world, the idea of wealth is often wrapped up in material things—bank balances, cars, houses, and promotions. But true wealth goes beyond possessions. The Bible says in **1 Timothy 6:10 (NIV)**, *"For the love of money is a root of all kinds of evil."* It's not money itself that's the problem; it's the **love of money**—the obsession with money, the drive to make it our ultimate goal—that becomes the trap. When money becomes our master, we lose sight of the real blessings God has for us. In my journey with Christ, I came to see that true wealth isn't about having a lot of things; it's about living in God's abundance. Through my growing relationship with God, I started seeing that no amount of money could give

> *When money becomes our master, we lose sight of the real blessings God has for us.*

me the security and joy that only God can provide. Even in the Bible, there are stories that teach us what real wealth looks like. Think of King Solomon, one of the wealthiest men in history. Solomon asked

God for a discerning heart to govern the people and to distinguish between right and wrong. He asked to be able to judge the people wisely. He didn't ask for wealth, and because his heart was aligned with God's will, God blessed him with riches beyond measure. Yet, in the end, Solomon realized that his wealth alone couldn't bring lasting fulfillment. **Ecclesiastes 5:10 (NIV)** records his reflection: "*Whoever loves money never has enough; whoever loves wealth is never satisfied with their income.*"

Consider Job, who lost everything—wealth, family, and health—but remained faithful to God. In the end, God restored him and blessed him with even more than he had before. Job's story is a powerful reminder that God is our true provider. When we cling to Him in faith, He is able to provide far beyond what we can imagine. This is real wealth: living with a heart surrendered to God, knowing that He is enough.

True wealth, as Myron Golden *(one of my favorite Christian entrepreneurs)* explains, isn't about stockpiling money—it's about adding value to others. God's blessing is designed not just to benefit us, but to flow through us to also bless others. When we live with this perspective, money becomes a tool, not the goal. The Bible reminds us in **Matthew 6:24** that we cannot serve both God and money. When money becomes an idol, we end up serving it, but when we serve God, money becomes a resource used for His glory.

If you're reading this and thinking, '*That sounds like me—I've been chasing money, striving for security, but still feeling empty,*' know that God wants to free you from that cycle. A poverty mindset isn't just about financial lack; it's a belief system that says we'll never have enough, that we'll never "arrive." This mindset keeps us from walking in the abundance God has for us, holding us back from the freedom and joy He intends. It also prevents us from fully living our lives on a daily basis since we are always thinking about some future time when things will finally work out for us. **Philippians 4:19 (NIV)** says, *"And my God will meet all your needs according to the riches of his glory in Christ Jesus."* God's provision isn't based upon our striving—it's based upon His love for us.

There was a point in my life where I had to intentionally start renewing my mind daily. I began replacing thoughts of scarcity and fear with the truth of God's Word. I realized that I didn't have to chase after money to find security; God is my source. He was with me through every hardship growing up, and He promises to be with me every step of the way. As I surrendered my finances, my fears, and my desire for "more" to Him, He began to shift my perspective. I learned to see wealth as more than possessions or bank balances; real wealth is found in knowing that God provides, in having peace and joy in Him, and in using what He's given me to be a blessing to others.

Biblical Principles for Breaking the Poverty Mindset and Living in Abundance

1. **Seek First God's Kingdom:** True wealth is found when we prioritize God over everything else. **Matthew 6:33 (NIV)** says, *"But seek first his kingdom and his righteousness, and all these things will be given to you as well."* When we put God first, He provides for our every need, teaching us that real security is found in Him.

2. **Renew Your Mind Daily:** Breaking a poverty mindset requires renewing our thoughts. **Romans 12:2 (NIV)** tells us, *"Do not conform to the pattern of this world, but be transformed by the renewing of your mind."* We need to replace thoughts of scarcity with God's promises, embracing the truth that He is our source.

3. **Trust in God's Provision, Not Money's Promise:** God wants us to trust Him for our provision, not the world's promises of wealth. **Philippians 4:19 (NIV)** reminds us, *"And my God will meet all your needs according to the riches of his glory in Christ Jesus."* True wealth is having peace, knowing God will supply all we need.

4. **Be Generous with What You Have:** Real wealth is rooted in generosity, knowing that what we have is a gift to be shared. **Proverbs 11:25 (NIV)** says, *"A generous person will prosper; whoever refreshes others will be refreshed."* True abundance grows when we freely give.

5. **Focus on Adding Value, Not Chasing Money:** Just like Myron Golden teaches, when we focus on adding value to others, God takes care of the rest. **2 Corinthians 9:8 (NIV)** encourages, *"And God is able to bless you abundantly, so that in all things at all times, having all that you need, you will abound in every good work."* This is true wealth, and it is measured not by what we accumulate but by the impact we have upon others.

If you've been on the endless chase, striving for more and feeling like it's never enough, know that God has a better way. Real wealth isn't about bank accounts or job titles; it's about peace, purpose, and knowing that every need you have is met in Christ. When we let go of the need to control, to strive, and to hoard, we open ourselves to receive the fullness of God's abundance.

Remember, the true test of wealth isn't in what we have, but in how we use what God has given us. God wants to set you free from any poverty mindset and bring you into a place of real abundance. This isn't the world's idea of "more, more, more," but a life of enough—

enough peace, enough joy, enough provision, and enough love to share with others.

You are loved, valued, and richly blessed by the One who owns it all. Live in the freedom of knowing that He is your source and provider. When you seek Him first, everything else falls into place.

A Prayer for Breaking the Poverty Mindset

Lord, I thank You for being my provider and teaching me that true wealth comes from You alone. Help me to renew my mind daily with Your truth, to break free from thoughts of scarcity, and to trust fully in Your provision. Teach me to live in true abundance, rooted in Your love, and to use what I have to bless others. May I walk confidently in Your promises, knowing that You are more than enough for me. In Jesus' name, Amen.

Chapter Eleven

CLEAR DECISIONS THROUGH GOD'S WISDOM – FINDING GUIDANCE IN CONFUSION

Let's be honest—making decisions is tough. Add in a dose of fear, a pinch of anxiety, and a sprinkle of confusion, and it's the perfect recipe for disaster. Have you ever been there? You know, that place where your heart feels pulled in a thousand directions, and your mind is clouded with doubts? It's in those moments that we're tempted to make quick decisions, hoping to just get it over with. Here's the thing: decisions made from a place of fear or uncertainty almost always lead to regret. **1 Corinthians 14:33 (ESV)** reminds us, *"For God is not a God of confusion but of peace."* His guidance brings us clarity, calm, and assurance.

When we rush into decisions without seeking His wisdom, it's like trying to navigate a stormy sea without a compass. However, when we wait on Him, when we lean into His peace, He provides the clarity we need to move forward with confidence. The Bible is full of examples of people who waited on God for direction—as well as examples of those who didn't. Spoiler alert: the ones who waited for divine direction came out a lot better!

A Biblical Example: Solomon Asks for Wisdom

When Solomon became king after his father, David, he faced a monumental challenge. He was young, inexperienced, and suddenly responsible for leading an entire nation. It would have been easy for Solomon to rely on the political advice of elders, the strategies of neighboring nations, or on his own limited understanding. However, Solomon knew that to make wise and clear decisions, he needed something greater—God's perspective.

In **1 Kings 3**, Solomon had a defining moment. God appeared to him in a dream and said, *"Ask for whatever you want me to give you"* **1 Kings 3:5 (NIV)**. Imagine having that kind of offer from the Creator of the universe. Solomon could have asked for riches, power, or even victory over his enemies—all the things that might seem logical for a king to desire. Instead, Solomon humbly acknowledged his limitations and asked for the ability to govern God's people wisely: *"So give your servant a discerning heart to govern your people and to distinguish between right and wrong"* **1 Kings 3:9 (NIV)**.

God was so pleased with Solomon's request that He not only granted him unparalleled wisdom but also blessed him with wealth and honor. Solomon's wisdom became legendary, and it enabled him to make decisions that brought peace and prosperity to his kingdom.

One of Solomon's most famous moments of wisdom—and let's admit, a bit of drama—came when two women who were prostitutes approached him with a baby, each claiming to be the mother. Just imagine the scene: tensions were high, emotions flaring, and Solomon sitting there thinking, *"How did I get stuck refereeing this?"* However, instead of losing his cool, he made what might be the most shocking decision ever suggested in a courtroom: *"Let's just cut the child in two and give each of you half."* **1 Kings 3:25 (NIV)** Of course, the real mother immediately spoke up, willing to give up her claim to save the child's life. Solomon's wild proposal wasn't about a final judgement—it was about exposing the truth.

This story isn't just a testament to Solomon's wisdom; it's a reminder of how God's wisdom can cut through even the most tangled and emotionally charged situations. So, the next time you're staring down a decision that feels impossible, remember Solomon—sometimes, all it takes is divine wisdom and a little creative problem-solving.

My Journey to Sell Our Home

I'll never forget the day I felt that nudge in my heart—it's time to sell the house. Let me paint the full picture for you: this wasn't just any house. This was the house. The house my boys and I had lived in for all of their lives. The house where countless memories had been made. At first, I brushed it off, thinking, *'surely this is just my own random thought. God wouldn't ask me to give away something He gifted to me, right?'* But as the day went on, the thought wouldn't leave. It was persistent, tugging at my heart until confusion and fear started to creep in.

I brought the decision to the Lord, but if I'm really honest, I wasn't ready to hear His answer. Selling the house? That wasn't even on my radar. It wasn't that I was overly attached to it; it was more the idea of letting go of something I knew God had gifted to me. How could I even consider giving away a blessing He had so clearly provided? The thought felt impossible, and I allowed this inner tug-of-war to stretch on for about a week.

Finally, I confided in a trusted friend, someone I deeply respect and who operates powerfully in the prophetic. Her response caught me completely off guard. With a look of relief, she said, "I'm so glad the Lord finally revealed that to you. I've been seeing the sale of your home for a while but didn't know how to bring it up." Her words hit me like a flood of confirmation, and in that moment, a wave of peace washed over me.

I realized that this wasn't about losing something precious; it was about stepping into something new. God wasn't taking something away—He was preparing me for the next chapter. If you're facing a decision that feels overwhelming or confusing, take heart. Sometimes what feels like a loss is actually an invitation to step into something far greater than you can imagine. Trust Him, lean into His peace, and know that His plans are always for your good **Romans 8:28**.

Sometimes what feels like a loss is actually an invitation to step into something far greater than you can imagine.

After that, I took it back to the Lord and waited for His guidance. This time, I felt absolute certainty. Even though the housing market wasn't great, and even though I didn't know where we would move or how it would all come together, I moved forward in faith. God even showed me a vision of the realtor I was supposed to use. Here's the kicker—it wasn't my sister, who is also a realtor! That was a tough decision, but I knew I had to be obedient and trust that God would take care of her too.

We prepped the house, listed it, and within 12 days, it sold for cash. I was speechless! Our yard guy even shared with me how other homes he serviced had been on the market for months with no offers. I knew only God could have orchestrated this.

Letting Go to Make Room for the New

God wasn't finished yet. After the house sold, I prayed and asked Him for help to pack up everything. I needed more than emotional strength; I needed tangible help. That's when I heard Him clearly say, *"You're not taking anything."* At first, I questioned it, wondering if I had misunderstood. Surely, He didn't mean everything. But those words settled in my heart, and I couldn't shake them.

That Saturday, during our neighborhood garage sale, I started selling off all our belongings—furniture, silverware, and everything in between. As I worked through the day, my realtor called. She said, "The new owner wants to buy everything—your furniture, dishes, all of it." I was stunned. In that moment, it all became clear. God hadn't just been asking me to let go of the house; He was helping me release the old to make room for something new.

It wasn't just about selling possessions—it was about trusting Him completely, even in the details I hadn't thought of. I realized this was the final piece in the process of stepping into the restoration God had been leading me towards. His faithfulness was evident in every step, reminding me that He truly does go before us and makes a way where there seems to be none.

If you're facing a moment where God is asking you to let go, know this: it's not about loss. It's about preparation. He's not just taking something away—He's clearing the way for what's next. Trust Him in the process, even when it's hard, because His plans are always for your good and His glory.

Biblical Principles for Making Decisions in Peace

1. **Wait for God's Peace:** If a decision feels rushed or is fueled by fear, it's not from God. His guidance always comes with peace.

Philippians 4:6-7 (NIV) reminds us, *"Do not be anxious about anything, but in every situation, by prayer and petition, with thanksgiving, present your requests to God. And the peace of God which transcends all understanding, will guard your hearts and your minds in Christ Jesus."*

2. **Seek Confirmation:** God often provides confirmation through His Word, through circumstances, or through trusted people in your life. Like Gideon, don't be afraid to ask Him for clarity and confirmation.

3. **Be Obedient, Even When It's Hard:** Obedience to God's leading may require sacrifices, but it also always leads to blessings. **Isaiah 1:19 (NIV)** says, *"If you are willing and obedient, you will eat the good things of the land."*

4. **Trust That God Has a Plan:** Even when you don't see the full picture, trust that God is already way ahead of you. **Proverbs 3:5-6 (NIV)** encourages, *"Trust in the LORD with all your heart and lean not on your own understanding; in all your ways submit to him, and he will make your paths straight."*

5. **Release Fear and Anxiety:** Fear is never a good guide for decision making. **2 Timothy 1:7 (NKJV)** reminds us, *"For God has not given us a spirit of fear, but of power and of love and of a sound mind."*

Moving Forward with Confidence

God's guidance is never rushed or chaotic. It comes with peace, clarity, and the assurance that He is in control. If you're facing a decision today, take a moment to pause. Seek His wisdom, wait for His peace, and trust that He will provide the clarity you need. Like Solomon, like me, and like so many others, you can walk forward in faith, knowing that God's plan is always good.

A Prayer for Wisdom in Decision-Making

Lord, I thank You that You are a God of peace and not confusion. Help me to bring every decision to You, trusting that You will guide me with clarity and wisdom. Teach me to wait for Your peace and to move forward in faith, knowing that You are always ahead of me, preparing the way. Thank You for Your love, Your provision, and Your faithfulness in every area of my life. In Jesus' name, Amen.

Chapter Twelve

VISION FOR TOMORROW – PURSUING GOD'S PATH FORWARD

Have you ever caught a glimpse of something bigger—something that stirs your heart and feels just out of reach? That's what it's like when God plants a vision inside of you. It's not just a random dream or a passing thought. It's a glimpse of His purpose for your life, calling you to step into something far greater than yourself.

But here's the thing about vision: it often comes long before we feel ready. It challenges us, stretches us, and requires faith to pursue. This chapter isn't about having all the answers—it's about trusting the One who does. **Proverbs 16:9** reminds us, *"In their hearts humans plan their course, but the LORD establishes their steps."* Even when the path ahead feels uncertain, God is guiding every step, weaving your story into something far greater than you can see.

Let's explore how to embrace the vision God has given you, how to navigate the trials and uncertainties that come with it, and how to stay anchored in His promises along the way. Whether you're standing at the edge of a dream or feeling stuck in the waiting, know this: God's vision for your life is worth pursuing. Let's take that leap of faith together.

Joseph's Journey into his Destiny

If anyone knew what it meant to persevere through trials and hold fast to a God-given vision, it was Joseph. His story, found in **Genesis chapters 37–50**, is one of the most inspiring examples of faith, resilience, and trusting in God's plan.

As a young man, Joseph received dreams from God that foretold his future. In these dreams, he saw himself in a position of authority, with his brothers bowing before him. Now, Joseph may have been a bit overzealous in sharing these dreams with his family, but the vision was clear: God had a great purpose for his life.

What followed, however, didn't look anything like the fulfillment of those dreams. Betrayed by his brothers, sold into slavery, falsely accused and imprisoned—Joseph's journey was filled with trial after trial. Yet through it all, Joseph didn't abandon the vision God had given him. He remained faithful, trusting that the God who gave him the dream would also bring it to pass.

Joseph's perseverance eventually paid off. God elevated him to the position of second-in-command in Egypt, where he not only saved the nation during a famine but also reconciled with his family. Joseph's story reminds us that God's plans often take time to unfold, and the journey to our destiny is rarely smooth. However, when we persevere, trusting God every step of the way, we'll see His promises fulfilled.

My Journey Into the Marketplace

This book is more than just words on a page—it's a step of faith into the marketplace for me. For years, I've received prophecy after prophecy about helping entrepreneurs find their footing, offering wisdom, and providing financing to those on the edge of something big. At first, these glimpses of my calling seemed so far from my current reality that I couldn't see how it could ever possibly happen. I didn't have the resources, the experience, or even the know how to step into the arena of the marketplace. Here's what I've learned: faith isn't about having all the answers—it's about trusting the One who does.

Writing this book is part of that trust. I believe it's a tool that will help countless entrepreneurs shake off hopelessness, see beyond their current circumstances, and walk boldly into their God-given destinies. It's not just about the practical tools or advice; it's about reigniting the belief that *"with God, all things are possible"* **Matthew 19:26 (NKJV)**.

If I can take this step of faith—into a space I know little about, with nothing but hope and His promises—you can too. Whether you're standing at the edge of a dream or in the middle of uncertainty, know this: God has equipped you for the journey ahead. He's not asking you to have it all figured out. He's simply asking you to trust Him, to take the first step, and to believe that He will meet you every step of the way.

You don't have to wait for the perfect moment, the perfect resources, or even the perfect confidence. Start where you are, with what you have, and let God lead you into the fullness of His plan. If He's called you to it, He will equip you for it. And when you feel like giving up, remember: faith is the bridge between where you are and where He's taking you.

This book is a testament to that faith, a declaration of hope for every entrepreneur, dreamer, and world changer waiting to step into their destiny. If I can do it, you can too. The time to step forward is now. The world is waiting for what God has placed inside of you. Take the step, trust the process, and watch as God turns your faith into something extraordinary.

Biblical Principles for Perseverance and Vision

1. **Trust God's Timing:** Joseph waited years for his dreams to come to pass, enduring trials that seemed to completely contradict the vision. **Habakkuk 2:3 (NIV)** reminds us, *"For the revelation [vision] is yet for an appointed time; it speaks of the end and will not prove false. Though it linger, wait for it; it will certainly come and will not delay."*

2. **Speak in Faith:** Like Joseph, we must declare God's promises over our lives, even when they seem impossible. **Romans 4:17 (NIV)** tells us about Abraham, *"He is our father in the sight of God, in whom he believed—the God who gives life to the dead and calls into being things that were not."*

3. **Stay Faithful in Small Things:** Joseph served faithfully in Potiphar's house, in prison, and wherever God placed him, preparing for the greater calling which lay ahead. **Luke 16:10 (NIV)** teaches, *"Whoever can be trusted with very little can also be trusted with much"*.

4. **Keep Your Eyes on the Bigger Picture:** Your purpose isn't just about you—it's about the people God will impact through you. **Galatians 6:9 (NIV)** encourages us, *"Let us not become weary in doing good, for at the proper time we will reap a harvest if we do not give up."*

5. **Find Strength in God's Promises:** Perseverance requires strength, and that strength comes from the promises of God. **Isaiah 40:31 (NIV)** declares, *"But those who hope in the Lord will renew their strength. They will soar on wings like eagles;*

they will run and not grow weary, they will walk and not be faint."

The Power of Knowing Your Purpose

When you know your purpose, it gives you a reason to keep going, even when the journey is hard. Joseph's vision sustained him through betrayal, slavery, and imprisonment. My calling into the marketplace pushes me to prepare, even when I don't have all the answers yet. Knowing your purpose allows you to pursue God's plan with confidence and excellence, trusting that He will equip you for everything He's called you to do.

When you know your purpose, it gives you a reason to keep going, even when the journey is hard.

Your purpose is not just for you; it's for the lives you're meant to touch, the hearts you're meant to inspire, and the change you're meant to bring into the world. Here's the beautiful part: God isn't asking you to do it alone. He's with you every step of the way, guiding you, strengthening you, and preparing the path ahead for you.

Walking Toward Your Destiny

If Joseph's story teaches us anything, it's that God's plans are worth the wait. Your current circumstances may not look like your destiny, but don't lose heart. Keep persevering, keep trusting, and keep speaking His promises over your life. Your trials are not the end of your story—they're the preparation for what's ahead.

As you move forward, remember this: God is faithful. He has equipped you with everything you need to fulfill your purpose, and He will not fail you. Walk boldly, speak in faith, and hold on to the vision He has given you. Your destiny is ahead, and it's more beautiful than you can imagine.

A Prayer for Perseverance and Vision

Father, I thank You for the vision You've placed in my heart. Help me to trust in Your timing, to persevere through trials, and to speak Your promises over my life daily. Give me the strength to walk boldly towards my destiny, knowing that You are faithful to fulfill every word You've spoken. Teach me to see beyond my current circumstances and to embrace the purpose You've called me to. Thank You for the hope, guidance, and grace You provide every step of the way. In Jesus' name, Amen.

Conclusion

The Best Is Yet to Come

Well, here we are—the end of this book, but far from the end of your journey. If you've made it to this point, let me first say: You're incredible! Secondly, let me remind you—this is only the beginning of what God has in store for you.

You've read the stories, absorbed the principles, and (hopefully) had a few laughs and felt a lot of hope along the way. Here's the truth: none of it matters if it just stays on these pages. The real "magic" happens when you get up, step out, and start walking towards the life God has prepared for you.

Hope Is Your Superpower

Life has a way of knocking us down, doesn't it? However, here's the truth: hope is what lifts us back up—not hope in the fleeting things of this world, but hope in the One who created it. Real hope isn't a fluffy, feel-good concept; it's a firm, unshakable belief that with God, the best is always yet to come. **Jeremiah 29:11 (NIV)** reminds us, *"For I know the plans I have for you... plans to prosper you and not to harm you, plans to give you hope and a future."*

This isn't just a promise for the good days when everything feels easy. It's a promise for the messy, chaotic, "I don't think I can handle one more thing" days. When life feels overwhelming, remember that your hope is in God—the One who holds your future in His hands. He isn't finished with your story yet. So, let this scripture be your rallying cry: Keep going, because the God who created you is faithful, and His plans for you are good.

Progress, Not Perfection

If you're waiting to "have it all together" before you move forward, let me stop you right there. No one has it all together. Progress isn't about perfection; it's about showing up, trusting God, and taking the next step. Baby steps count. Wobbly steps count. Heck, even crawling counts if that's where you are today. A very wise man once told me that perfectionism waits for the perfect moment, while excellence creates it!

Let's be real—sometimes, you'll take two steps forward and one step back. That's okay. Grace was made for that. The important thing is to just keep moving, trusting that God will guide your path, even if you can't see the whole picture yet.

Laugh a Little

Can I just say something? Take a deep breath. Yes, right now. Do it. Life is serious enough without you adding unnecessary pressure to yourself. Learn to laugh—at your mistakes, at the unexpected detours, and sometimes even at how ridiculous things can get. You know God has a sense of humor; just look at how He uses imperfect people to do extraordinary things.

The Hope You Carry

Here's what I want you to remember as you close this book: the hope inside of you isn't just for you. It's for the people around you—the family, the friends, and even the strangers who need a little light in their darkness. You don't have to be perfect to share it; you just have to be willing.

God has placed a unique purpose upon your life, one that only you can fulfill. So, when it feels like the weight of the world is on your shoulders, remember: you're not carrying it alone. God is with you, and He is more than enough.

A Prayer as You Step Forward

Lord, I thank You for the journey You've brought us on through these pages. I pray for the one reading this right now, that they would feel Your presence and know Your peace. Strengthen their heart, renew their hope, and remind them of the beautiful purpose You've placed on their life. May they walk boldly into the future You've prepared for them, trusting that the best is always yet to come. Amen.

So, my friend, this is where I leave you, but it's not the end of the story. It's the beginning of your next chapter. You have everything you need to move forward: a God who loves you, a hope that sustains you, and a story that's still unfolding. Now go, live boldly, love deeply, and never stop believing that with God, anything is possible.

Don't forget—keep laughing along the way. Life is better that way.

Until we meet again,

Maria

About the Author

Maria Watkins is a devoted follower of Jesus whose faith journey over the past eight years has transformed her life and given her purpose. As a loving mother to two Godly young men, she finds her greatest joy in nurturing their spiritual growth and guiding them to walk boldly in their faith and God-given callings.

Maria's academic accomplishments reflect her dedication to excellence and lifelong learning. She holds a Bachelor's degree in Computer Engineering, an Associate's degree in Design and Redesign, and has also graduated from Bible College with proficiency in Financial Stewardship. She has also completed RIG University for both of the Prophetic and Apostolic terms with excellence, deepening her understanding of Kingdom principles and her commitment to serving others through her God-given calling.

With a heart for empowering others, Maria is passionate about helping families, particularly those of single women, to embrace their divine destinies. Through her wisdom, encouragement, and unwavering faith, she seeks to inspire others to live boldly in their purpose and walk fully in God's promises. Her life is a testament to resilience, faith, and a deep commitment to seeing others flourish in all that God has planned for them.